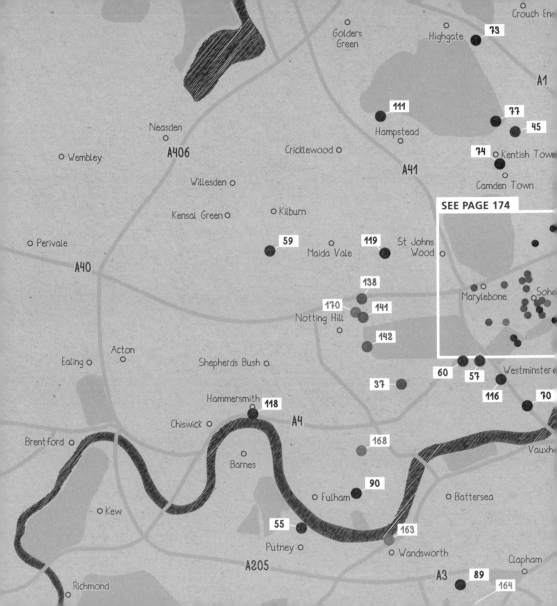

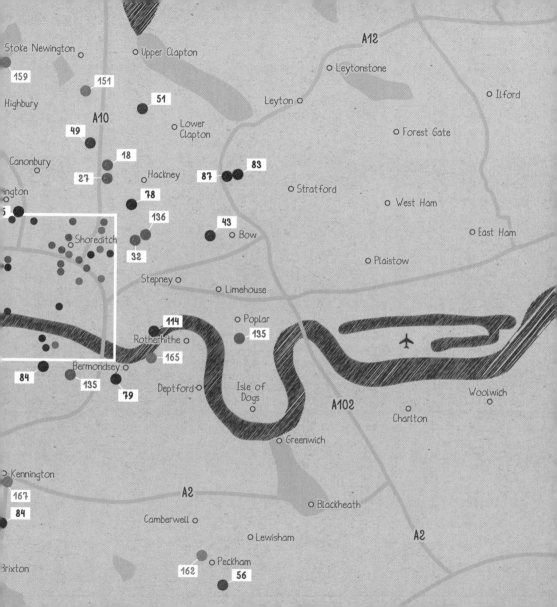

DRINK LONDON

THE 100 BEST BARS AND PUBS

EUAN FERGUSON

PHOTOGRAPHS BY KIM LIGHTBODY

WHITE LION
PUBLISHING

CONTENTS

MAP · 2
INTRODUCTION · 9

COCKTAILS ● 11

LEGENDARY LOCALS ● 39

CRAFT BEER, ALE & CIDER ● 63

LIQUID HISTORY ● 93

WINE & SPIRITS SPECIALISTS ● 121

WITH A TWIST ● 145

TICK INDEX · 172
CENTRAL LONDON MAP · 174

INTRODUCTION

What makes a great bar or pub? Personal service, fancy fixtures and furnishings, cutting-edge cocktails? Or a familiar welcome, well-cellared ales, a real fire? Somewhere to set the pulse racing or somewhere quiet to escape to? There's really no single answer.

With more than 7,000 licensed premises in London, no one's going to go thirsty, but the choice can be bewildering. Given too that they're all spread over an area of 600 square miles, it makes the simple act of going for a drink a bit complicated. But this is your guide, no matter what the occasion: a date that needs impressing, a party of pals who need entertaining, an out-of-towner who needs a tour of the city's ancient or eccentric watering holes, or simply an afternoon that needs whiling away in peace and quiet. And there's no 'not bad' or 'it'll do' – from the thousands of contenders in every corner of the capital, these are the 100 best, each one unique, memorable or unrivalled at what they do.

Think of this book as a helpful, knowledgeable (and sociable) friend, someone who always knows the perfect answer to that age-old question: where shall we go for a drink?

COCKTAILS

LONDON COCKTAIL CLUB • 14

EXPERIMENTAL COCKTAIL CLUB • 14

COCKTAIL LOUNGE AT THE

ZETTER TOWNHOUSE • 17

UNTITLED • 18

SUPER LYAN • 20

MILK & HONEY • 20

COBURG BAR AT THE CONNAUGHT • 22

PUNCH ROOM • 23

BAR AMÉRICAIN • 24

THREE SHEETS • 27

MARK'S BAR • 29

NIGHTJAR • 30

HAPPINESS FORGETS • 31

COUPETTE • 32

HAWKSMOOR • 34

WORSHIP STREET WHISTLING SHOP • 36

SWIFT • 36

SCOUT • 37

COCKTAILS

London is the cocktail capital of the world. Its stars behind the bar never stand still, continually innovating and challenging perceptions of what it's possible to do with a shelf of spirits, a shaker and a few ice cubes. Places like Scout and Nightjar incorporate all sorts of homemade and high-tech ingredients in their original creations, but it's not all about molecular mixology and the appliance of science. Some say the peak of the bartender's skill is the classic cocktail – Sazeracs, Manhattans, Daquiris – and in London they're made better than anywhere else. Don't forget either about the many five-star hotel bars in the city. It's a common misconception that you have to be either rich or a guest (or both) to drink in the likes of the Savoy, the Connaught or the Goring, but for the price of a cocktail anyone can be treated like royalty for an hour or so. It's an experience to be tried at least once.

comes with a dippable marshmallow.
61 Goodge Street, Fitzrovia, W1T 1TL.
☎ *020 7580 1960*
🖳 *www.londoncocktailclub.co.uk*
⊖ *Goodge Street tube. Branches at Bethnal
Green, Covent Garden, Islington, Liverpool Street,
Monument, Oxford Circus, Shaftesbury Avenue,
Shoreditch.*

● EXPERIMENTAL COCKTAIL CLUB

**Drink... vintage spirits that are probably older
than you.**
Scents of barbecued duck and aniseed turn the heads
of Chinatown tourists, but those in the know head
straight to a scuffed and anonymous door at No 13a.
It leads into one of the most secretive of London's
bars, a dimly lit den of cocktail extravagance. A bit of
sweet-talk directed the doorman's way is sometimes
required if you've not booked, but a treat awaits once
inside – the drinks are among the most distinguished
in the city. Further excitement: there's a cabinet
of vintage spirits, including 1950s Martell XO and
twentieth-century gins. Experimental Cocktail Club
is hard to find, hard to get into, even harder to leave.
ESSENTIAL ORDER A Vintage Purgatory
(1951 Old Overholt rye, 1950s Benedictine,
1970s chartreuse).
13a Gerrard Street, Chinatown, W1D 5PS.
🖳 *www.chinatownecc.com*
⊖ *Piccadilly Circus tube.*

● LONDON COCKTAIL CLUB

**Drink... in a high-spirited saturnalia of
cocktail celebration.**
Some bars are about exclusivity, refinement,
multisensory creations which push the boundaries
of mixology. But not London Cocktail Club. It's a
place to simply forget the cruel world outside, letting
your hair down and have a whole load of fun. The
decor's loud, the music's loud, the crowd's loud and
the cocktails aren't shy either. A comprehensive list
covers everything from a Cuba Libre to the more out-
there Bacon & Egg Martini: a real liquid lunch.
A great place to lose an evening.
ESSENTIAL ORDER The pudding-like The Dude

● COCKTAIL LOUNGE AT THE ZETTER TOWNHOUSE

Drink... in a curiosity shop of a cocktail bar.

It's that easy to get carried away in here. Like an auction house storeroom magically arranged into a bar, Zetter Townhouse is an endlessly fascinating mishmash of furniture, taxidermy (look for the boxing kangaroo), porcelains, paintings, portraits and assorted *objets d'art*. There are numerous studded sofas to squish into, but sit at the bar to watch the action as the friendly staff create dainty cocktails (the prices are pleasant too). It's overseen by Tony Conigliaro, something of a legend on the London bar scene.

ESSENTIAL ORDER The Flintlock illustrates the Zetter's creativity and theatre: gin, gunpowder tea tincture, sugar, dandelion and burdock bitters, and Fernet Branca, served with a bang...

49–50 St John's Square, Farringdon, EC1V 4JJ.
☎ *020 7324 4545*
🖳 *www.thezettertownhouse.com*
⊖ *Farringdon tube.*

● UNTITLED

Drink... cocktails made of clay.
Some of the ingredients on the cocktail list at this science-driven bar will raise eyebrows with their enigmatic descriptions – 'Snow' contains white clay, chalk and enoki vodka, for example – but trust that you're in safe hands and pick something that takes your fancy. Untitled is another project by master mixologist Tony Conigliaro, and it's his most avant-garde yet. Looking more like an art gallery than a bar, with polished concrete everywhere and striking design touches, it is the result of years of experience of experimenting and perfecting with flavour to create drinks that are not only wildly inventive but also keep you coming back.

ESSENTIAL ORDER The cocktail menu changes every few months, but try the Rye if you can: it's like a deeper, smoother Old Fashioned, with toasted rye syrup and rye bitters.

538 Kingsland Road, Dalston, E8 4AH.
☎ *07841 022924*
🖥 *www.untitled-bar.com*
⊖ *Dalston Junction Overground.*

● SUPER LYAN

Drink... the mind-melting concoctions of a bartending superstar.

Ryan Chetiyawardana, aka Mr Lyan, shook the London cocktail scene to its core with the opening of White Lyan on this same site, a former pub in Hoxton. It had no branded bottles, no ice, no fruit, and it freaked out the squares; he closed it at its peak, then opened the swankier Dandelyan. Now it's back, with pioneering no-waste restaurant Cub

upstairs, and this equally sharp bar in the basement. The cocktails are maybe less radical than before – there are brands, ice and fruit – but you'll still be drinking things that combine the everyday with the fantastical (the Bloodshot Negroni has bourbon, Campari, beef tea, vermouth and mandarin spritz).

ESSENTIAL ORDER The Army & Navy is a zesty treat with gin, cobnut syrup and grapefruit spray.

155 Hoxton Street, Hoxton, N1 6PJ.
☎ *020 3011 1153* 🖥 *www.superlyan.com*
⊖ *Hoxton Overground.*

● MILK & HONEY

Drink... in the dark.

Visitors here make much of the lack of light in this multifloor Soho cocktail hideaway. It certainly is dim, although far from dingy. When your eyes adjust you'll make out a small but smart bar with Prohibition-era design touches, and nattily dressed barman pouring some of the meanest cocktails in London. They sound unshowy – straightforward lists of spirits with no mention of brands – but they're consistently and precisely made. Note: it's mostly members only, although the rest of us can visit until 11pm (by reservation only, but it's worth it).

ESSENTIAL ORDER The list is long, but try a London Calling: gin, sherry, lemon, sugar, bitters.

61 Poland Street, Soho, W1F 7NU.
☎ *020 7065 6800* 🖥 *www.mlkhny.com*
⊖ *Oxford Circus tube.*

● COBURG BAR AT THE CONNAUGHT

Drink... in the city's most charming hotel bar.

The imposing Regency edifice of the Connaught is quite the landmark in this villagey part of Mayfair, and it comes with two world-class bars: there's not much in terms of appeal to separate the Coburg Bar (a subtly modern and warm update of an old room) from the Connaught Bar (sleeker, shimmeringly opulent). The Connaught has a mobile martini trolley, but the Coburg has an incredible cocktail menu, a chronological catalogue of classics. There are also dozens of gins, vodkas and rums, and bottlers'-edition cask whiskies; the champagne list is one of the most outstanding in London. If you've bagged a seat, raise a glass.

ESSENTIAL ORDER From the 1800s to contemporary creations, every cocktail is flawless.

The Connaught, Carlos Place, Mayfair, W1K 2AL.
☎ *020 7499 7070*
🖥 *www.the-connaught.co.uk*
⊖ *Green Park tube.*

● PUNCH ROOM

Drink... the oldest mixed drinks in the world.

The Lobby Bar in the swanky Edition hotel is a sumptuously appointed Regency wonder with lofty ceilings and a chattering crowd, but through the back is the dark, discreet and clubby Punch Room, a reservations-only room specialising in the ancient drink of choice of pirates and privateers, first brought to the West in the 1600s. Settle into a plush leather armchair and peruse the concise list, which ranges from tropical blends made with coconut and angostura to homegrown versions flavoured with oak moss syrup and tea.

ESSENTIAL ORDER The potent and tangy Oxford Punch, with port, cognac, rum, green tea, lemon sherbet and orange sherbet.

London Edition, 10 Berners Street, Fitzrovia, W1T 3NP.
☎ *020 7781 0000*
🖥 *www.editionhotels.com*
⊖ *Tottenham Court Road tube.*

● BAR AMÉRICAIN

Drink... in a 1930s bar that puts Prohibition-era pretenders to shame.

Right next to touristy Piccadilly Circus, the basement of the former Regent Palace Hotel has undergone a few transformations since it opened in 1915; its current incarnation makes it one of the most spectacular cocktail bars in London. The beaux arts decor is indeed beautiful, with repeated airplane motifs and woodblock pillars – it benefitted from the cream of the early twentieth century's art deco design expertise, and makes the most of it today. But anyone can walk in off the street attired however they choose and partake of the truly excellent cocktails.

ESSENTIAL ORDER The classics are consummate, the original creations better.

Try something from the 'house cocktails' list.

20 Sherwood Street, Soho, W1F 7ED.

☎ *020 7734 4888*

🖳 *www.brasseriezedel.com/bar-americain*

⊖ *Piccadilly Circus tube.*

● THREE SHEETS

Drink... in a pared-back bar that's all about ten-out-of-ten drinks.
A neighbourhood hangout with all the right ingredients: a laidback atmosphere (with a tendency to turn into a lively one); convivial seating at the bar; and a short, simple menu designed by brothers Max and Noel Venning. They've arranged the menu to move from 'one sheet' (light, fresh cocktails) to 'three sheets' (more robust), and included ferments, cordials and other pre-prepped batched ingredients for a seasonal touch.
ESSENTIAL ORDER French 75 – a batched and bottled take on the classic cocktail (gin, champagne and lemon) poured straight from a chilled bottle.
510b Kingsland Road, Dalston, E8 4AE.
☎ *07718 648771*
🖥 *www.threesheets-bar.com*
⊖ *Dalston Junction Overground.*

● MARK'S BAR

Drink... your way around Britain.

Chef Mark Hix, whose flagship restaurant is on the ground floor, is a proud proponent of cooking with seasonal, British, seldom-seen ingredients. This effortlessly cool and clubby bar in the basement does the same with its cocktails. Redcurrant syrup, Burrow Hill Farm cider, sea buckthorn – even green pea-infused London dry gin and atholl brose (Scottish oatmeal dessert) appear in the stunning concoctions. There are also Hix's own beers, a great wine list and some first-rate bar snacks (scotched quail's eggs, for instance). All round, one of the most agreeable places to drink in London.

ESSENTIAL ORDER The Hix Fix is a modern classic – Somerset apple eau de vie, morello cherry and sparkling English wine.

66–70 Brewer Street, Soho, W1F 9UP.
☎ *020 7292 3518* ▭ *www.marksbar.co.uk*
⊖ *Piccadilly Circus tube.*

● **NIGHTJAR**

Drink... through the jazz age.
This is how to ace a trend without jumping on
the bandwagon. Nightjar is the closest London
has to the sort of place Al Capone might have
demanded protection money from in 1920s
Chicago. There's live jazz most nights, waistcoated
staff, seriously low levels of lighting and a
completely unmarked entrance on a grotty bit
of east London road. But standards are so high
that every night out here is special. Is there a more
inventive and appealing-sounding cocktail list
in London? A more accommodating welcome?
It's doubtful.
ESSENTIAL ORDER The drinks list reaches a peak
with the Toronto: bourbon, roasted pecan maple
syrup, Fernet Branca and orange blossom candy floss.
129 City Road, Shoreditch, EC1V 1JB.
☎ *020 7253 4101*
🖳 *www.barnightjar.com*
⊖ *Old Street tube.*

● HAPPINESS FORGETS

Drink... in a memorably brilliant bar.
Hoxton has come a long way from when it was
the coolest area of London: you have to hunt out
the great places out these days. And here's one of
the greatest, right in the former hipster nucleus
of Hoxton Square, down an unmarked stairway,
below a restaurant – it's a dark, tiny, unelaborately
furnished and ultra-classy operation that always
gets everything right. Superior cocktails, ultra-
smooth service, happy people: visit once and
you'll never forget it.
ESSENTIAL ORDER The Perfect Storm exemplifies
the cleverly modified classics on the menu –
dark rum, honey, lemon and ginger juice and
plum brandy.
8–9 Hoxton Square, Hoxton, N1 6NU.
🖥 *www.happinessforgets.com*
⊖ *Old Street tube.*

● **COUPETTE**

Drink... the French way.
Picon bière, calvados, cognac, armagnac, cidre, liqueur, and of course all that wine... France may be most famous for its food, but its drinks hold up pretty well too. Coupette was opened in 2017 by former Savoy (see p100) head bartender Chris Moore, and it celebrates all that's good from over the Channel (there is food too, mainly the pleasingly uncomplicated likes of croque-monsieur or charcuterie). All that Savoy knowledge hasn't gone to waste – the French-accented cocktails are incredible, but exploring the long list of non-mixed French drinks is just as fun.
ESSENTIAL ORDER The champagne piña colada, with coconut sorbet and Moët & Chandon, is causing quite a stir.
423 Bethnal Green Road,
Bethnal Green, E2 0AN.
☎ *0207 7299 562*
▭ *www.coupette.co.uk*
⊖ *Bethnal Green tube.*

● HAWKSMOOR

Drink... where the steaks are high class and the cocktails rarefied.

Hawksmoor is known for its sensational cuts of best-of-British beef, but downstairs (in what was once a Russian strip club) at its Spitalfields branch is an always-lively bar which serves drinkers as well as diners. It looks timeless, but the fittings are all cleverly salvaged; the wall tiles, for instance, came from a St James's hotel lift shaft.

Cocktails are witty and excellent: five special drinks are chosen monthly by one of Hawksmoor's talented bartenders.

ESSENTIAL ORDER Shaky Pete's Ginger Brew: a modern classic with ginger syrup, lemon, gin and London Pride ale.

157a Commercial Street, Spitalfields, E1 6BJ.
☎ *020 7426 4856* 🖥 *www.thehawksmoor.com*
⊖ *Shoreditch High Street Overground.*
Branches at Air Street, Borough, Guildhall, Knightsbridge, Seven Dials.

● WORSHIP STREET WHISTLING SHOP

Drink... in a Dickensian cocktail laboratory.
'Coriander and black pepper hydrosol', 'raspberry and mustard cordial', 'banana and clove vinegar'... These are not ordinary ingredients to find behind the bar, but WSWS is no ordinary bar. In a corner of this dark and enigmatic basement in a quiet part of Shoreditch there's a high-tech set-up involving a distilling machine, a water bath and a liquid-nitrogen freezer; if science leaves you baffled, simply sit safe in the knowledge that it results in some of the most fabulous drinks in town.
ESSENTIAL ORDER The signature Black Cats, with Tanqueray, vermouth, 'removed cream' (ask for the

elaborate explanation) and a radish garnish.
63 Worship Street, Shoreditch, EC2A 2DU.
☎ *020 7247 0015* 🖳 *www.whistlingshop.com*
⊖ *Liverpool Street tube.*

● SWIFT

Drink... in an upstairs-downstairs bar for every in-town occasion.
Cocktail bar royalty clubbed together to launch Swift (that's talent from Nightjar, p30, and Milk & Honey, p20). The result is as slick and thoughtful as you'd hope. There's a glossy art deco-inspired bar on the ground floor where you might perch on a stool for a quick Sgroppino (lemon sorbet, prosecco); downstairs there's a romantically lit den with

intimate booths and a more expansive cocktail menu that features drinks with more storm and depth.
ESSENTIAL ORDER Praline Flip (downstairs) – a very grown up pudding, comprising a Swift-spiced rum, Guinness and hazelnut orgeat.
12 Old Compton Street, Soho, W1D 4TQ.
☎ *020 7437 7820* 🖥 *www.barswift.com*
⊖ *Tottenham Court Road tube.*

● SCOUT

Drink... with the seasons.
Classic cocktails are called classic for a reason: they've been on menus for decades, year-in, year-out. But a new way of drinks-making is emerging across the world: one that mirrors the restaurant world and emphasises sustainability, seasonality and ingredient-sourcing. At Scout, a very composed bar with a handsome Scandi look, this means a menu with cocktails sporting names like 'Hay', or 'Cedarwood', and containing unusual ingredients like hogweed kombucha, or false acacia, or spruce. There are home-brewed beers, and a section devoted to ferments made with house yeasts, which taste intriguingly like natural wines. One for cocktail adventurers.
ESSENTIAL ORDER Forget all about the cocktails you're used to and ask to be surprised. You will be.
93 Great Eastern Street, Shoreditch, EC2A 3HZ.
☎ *020 7686 8225* 🖥 *www.scout.bar*
⊖ *Old Street tube.*

LEGENDARY LOCALS

THE QUEEN'S HEAD • 42

THE LORD TREDEGAR • 43

THE PINEAPPLE • 45

THE CHARLES LAMB • 45

THE WENLOCK ARMS • 46

THE RAILWAY TAVERN ALE HOUSE • 49

THE CLAPTON HART • 51

THE CARPENTER'S ARMS • 52

THE BRICKLAYER'S ARMS • 55

THE IVY HOUSE • 56

THE GRENADIER • 57

PARADISE BY WAY OF KENSAL GREEN • 59

THE NAG'S HEAD • 60

LEGENDARY LOCALS

Every Londoner, from Wimbledon to Walthamstow, has a local. And every Londoner thinks their local is the best. In a way, they're right: when it comes to drinking there's a time for excitement and a time for familiarity, and familiarity is what you get in your favourite neighbourhood pub. It's unlikely that everyone knows your name, or that your order's being poured as soon as you're through the door; but maybe a nod of recognition from the landlord, a favourite seat by the fire, a pat for the pub dog and a short walk home at the end of the night is enough. Even if you're not propping up the bar every night (not recommended, of course), it's comforting to know it's there. But some locals are worth a visit even if you don't live nearby. These are places that bring something different to the backstreets and 'villages' of London – a brilliant beer selection, say (the The Bricklayer's Arms), or a family-friendly spirit (Paradise by Way of Kensal Green), or that indefinable good feeling you get as soon as you enter (all of these following places). Some of them are so good that you might be glancing speculatively in estate agents' windows after you leave, wondering if a good local is reason enough to move house.

● THE QUEEN'S HEAD

Drink... in 'the best pub in London'.
...or so a sign outside states. A claim too far, maybe, but the Queen's Head is a very noble proposition all the same. The streets around the great stations are generally uninspiring in pub terms, which makes this cosy and friendly place near King's Cross stand out even more. Preserving many of its original Victorian features, it's run by a genuine beer and cider devotee who changes the casks and kegs on offer regularly, and his onsite microbrewery began operation in 2014. What's more, there's a piano – nothing says 'local' like a singalong.

ESSENTIAL ORDER It's an award-winning cider pub – there's always a couple of artisan varieties on the bar.

66 Acton Street, King's Cross, WC1X 9NB.
☎ *020 7713 5772*
🖥 *www.queensheadlondon.com*
⊖ *King's Cross tube.*

● THE LORD TREDEGAR

Drink... in Mile End's finest pub for miles around.
There aren't many of these mid-terrace Georgian
pubs left in London – most of them have been
turned into residences – so three cheers for the
Lord T, an exceptionally tasteful remodelled old
hostelry in an East End conservation area not far
from Victoria Park. Anyone would be delighted to
have such a pleasing place within walking distance
of home – it's beautifully balanced between a
handsome front bar area, a conservatory beside
the open kitchen at the back, and a side room
with a wall-size map of the world where you can
sit and plan your next holiday. Take some coins for
the '60s jukebox.
ESSENTIAL ORDER Look out for the sparky
and thirst-quenching Litovel lager on tap, imported
from the Czech Republic.
50 Lichfield Road, Bow, E3 5AL.
☎ *020 8983 0130* ⊖ *Mile End tube.*

● THE PINEAPPLE

Drink... in a backstreet boozer you'll want to come back to again and again.

In an area embarrassingly rich with good pubs, the Pineapple stands head-and-shoulders above the rest, and not just for its wonderful throwback name (imagine how exotic the spiky fruit must have seemed to Victorians used to domestic damsons and plain old plums). Thanks to motivated locals it survived an attempt in the early 2000s to develop it into apartments. It's an easygoing place that's at once convivial, cosy or comforting, suiting drinkers sociable and solitary alike; Kentish Towners are kept busy here with live comedy, a fiendish quiz, seasonal singalongs and a cheese-celebration night called... Cheese Night.

ESSENTIAL ORDER There's usually a real ale from Tottenham's Redemption to tuck in to.
51 Leverton Street, Kentish Town, NW5 2NX.
☎ *020 7284 4631* ⊖ *Kentish Town tube.*

● THE CHARLES LAMB

Drink... in a Gallic interpretation of a London pub.

A tasteful edit of a dinky corner site in a desirable part of Islington has resulted in a quality pub with a mild French accent. It's an entente cordiale that works well: there are English ales, like Darkstar from Sussex, plus Breton cider; a blackboard advertises the 'Liste des vins', a sign proclaims 'Good people drink good beer', and cockerel motifs strut around. A wonderful little place.

ESSENTIAL ORDER A French aperitif is practically de rigueur – a Picon biere, which is orange bitters mixed with lager, is perfect.
16 Elia Street, Islington, N1 8DE.
☎ *020 7837 5040* 🖥 *www.thecharleslambpub.com*
⊖ *Angel tube.*

● THE WENLOCK ARMS

Drink... in a little pub that took on big business and won.

It could have been depressingly familiar. When this treasured public house came under threat of redevelopment into flats in 2010, it seemed the writing was on the wall. But regulars weren't having it: a conservation order was won from Hackney Council, and against all odds this old pub was saved and, some might say, came back stronger. It's everything you want in a London boozer – great beer, simple food, loyal locals. It's the sort of place that warms your heart just to walk past it; go inside and you'll be very glad you did. Quite possibly the best pub in London.

ESSENTIAL ORDER The huge range of ales and ciders demands your attention.

26 Wenlock Road, Hoxton, N1 7TA.
☎ *020 7608 3406*
🖥 *www.wenlockarms.com*
⊖ *Old Street tube.*

LONDON TRANSPORT-

- ASH GROVE MARE STREET
- CLAPTON KENNINGHALL ROAD
- FINSBURY PARK STATION
- STOKE NEWINGTON
- WHITECHAPEL LONDON HOSPITAL

● THE RAILWAY TAVERN
ALE HOUSE

Drink... in a midcentury station waiting room.
In a Georgian back street on the Islington/Hackney
borders, an old pub was given back its proper
name in 2012 along with a subtle sprucing up to
emphasise its handsome 1950s features. Now, it
brings to mind somewhere JB Priestley might settle
into for an afternoon half and the crossword while
his driver waits outside. The vintage Underground art
and carriage-compartment-brown wood transports
you to a gentler age; the superbly kept ales and craft
beers bring you pleasantly back up to date. Visit after
a dispiriting twenty-first-century commute.
ESSENTIAL ORDER A pint of something dark
and fortifying served in a proper dimpled and
handled pint glass.
2–4 St Jude Street, Dalston, N16 8JT.
☎ *020 3092 3344* ● *Dalston Kingsland Overground.*

● THE CLAPTON HART

Drink... in a haunted junk shop.
Taking the bric-a-brac-chic look to a new level, this immense and imposing pub has almost every inch of its bare plaster walls, floors and ceilings adorned with bits and pieces picked up and repurposed as decoration: de-strung pianos turned into tables, found furnishings, colourful bunting, old prints and other motley items to constantly catch the eye. This northern part of Hackney is very much on-the-up, and the Hart's arty aesthetic suits it superbly.
ESSENTIAL ORDER The dedication to local craft beers is commendable – try one of the many now brewed in the borough.
231 Lower Clapton Road,
Clapton, E5 8EG.
☎ *020 8985 8124*
🖳 *www.claptonhart.com*
⊖ *Clapton rail.*

● THE CARPENTER'S ARMS

Drink... in the Krays' mum's old pub.

The story goes that this comely corner site was owned by the mother of the notorious East End gangsters (their portrait's on the wall). It's a lesson in how to bring a Victorian pub up to date, bringing in a bit of modern style while preserving character. And what makes it special? On-hand owners keeping an eye on things, globetrotting beers, classy wines, a big flower display, candlesticks, chandeliers. Locals swear by it and you will too –

it's rare to find somewhere this personal so close to the relentless Brick Lane.

ESSENTIAL ORDER The twins were apparently partial to a G & T, but do you really want to be like them? The chalked-up wine list has an admirable selection of Old and New World varieties available by the glass.

73 Cheshire Street, Whitechapel, E2 6EG.
☎ *020 7739 6342*
🖥 *www.carpentersarmsfreehouse.com*
⊖ *Whitechapel tube.*

● THE BRICKLAYER'S ARMS

Drink... in a coal-fired classic pub where the real ale's the real deal.
When it opened in 1862, this unassuming backstreet pub was known as the Waterman's Arms, given that it's just a couple of lengths from the river; when building houses became London's main manufacturing activity in late Victorian times it was given its current name. It has remained so ever since, with various ups and downs, but now it's on a triumphant up. More cask ale taps than a beer festival, a real coal fire for the winter, a garden for the summer, an indoor skittles alley for when the beer isn't enough (or you've had too much). **ESSENTIAL ORDER** A dark, swirling English ale in winter, a light, hoppy one in summer.
32 Waterman Street, Putney, SW15 1DD.
☎ *020 8785 4344*
🖥 *www.bricklayers-arms.co.uk*
⊖ *Putney Bridge tube.*

● **THE IVY HOUSE**

Drink... in a pub that could start a revolution.
A sprawling 1930s Truman's tavern on an
unprepossessing residential street near Peckham
Rye... not much would suggest the Ivy House was
worthy of attention, but it's a real trailblazer. Locals
came together in 2012 to form a cooperative to save
the building from redevelopment; in a model that
could be copied all over the country, it reopened in
2013 as the first community-owned pub in Britain.
It's now a genuine Nunhead hub: real ales, a kitchen
serving good food, and a space for the likes of yoga,
live music, theatre and storytelling.
ESSENTIAL ORDER Several London breweries are
shareholders of the Ivy House. Show your support
and plump for one.
40 Stuart Road, Nunhead, SE15 3BE.
☎ *020 7277 8233*
🖥 *www.ivyhousenunhead.com*
⊖ *Nunhead rail.*

● THE GRENADIER

Drink… in the Foot Guards' watering hole.
There's a sense of achievement that comes with
finding this slightly unexpected Belgravia boozer:
it's up and round the corner of a private mews
running from a side street off a majestic stuccoed
square. You're not going to stumble across it, that's
for sure. Tourists lap up the history – it was built
in 1720 to house a local army regiment – and in
summer drinkers spill out on to the street among
the flowers and fancy cars of Wilton Row. Out of
season it's a secluded spot, with a handsome pewter
bar, horsey memorabilia, a fire and loads of bay-
brown wood.

ESSENTIAL ORDER Adnams Broadside was
brewed to celebrate a British military victory –
it's a rich, ruby-red ale.
18 Wilton Row, Belgravia, SW1X 7NR.
☎ *020 7235 3074*
⊖ *Hyde Park Corner tube.*

● PARADISE BY WAY OF KENSAL GREEN

Drink... in heaven just off the Harrow Road.
Imagine a licensed version of Miss Havisham's
Satis House in Great Expectations, relocated from
Kent to Kensal Rise, and you're not far off this hugely
popular please-all pub. The shabby-chic, taxidermy-
heavy decor in the main bar is punctuated by
religious iconography; there's also a restaurant,
a club/performance space, two gardens, a library
and other nooks and crannies used for flea markets,
DJs, bands, comedy and cabaret. This means it
draws a broad a range of people, including families,
groups out for Sunday roast (the pillowy Yorkshire
puds are fantastic), boozy-brunchers, clubbers and
weekend paper readers.
ESSENTIAL ORDER The Bloody Mary is
justifiably famous, and it's not just for hangovers.
19 Kilburn Lane, Kensal Green, W10 4AE.
☎ *020 8969 0098* 🖥 *www.theparadise.co.uk*
⊖ *Kensal Green tube.*

● THE NAG'S HEAD

Drink... in the Duke of Westminster's local.
Two minutes' walk from the luxe-max Berkeley hotel, past the Range Rovers and starched-shirt-white mews flats, is this incongruous anachronism, a knick-knack-filled retreat from the real world with an interior the same brown as a comfy old pair of slippers. There's a ruthlessly enforced ban on mobiles, so you can hear the quiet retro jazz and murmur of the contemplative pint sippers. But you'd have to be lucky or rich to call this pub your local. The rent is paid to the Duke of Westminster, one of Britain's richest men: the Nag's Head is far from aristocratic, but it's still a class act.

ESSENTIAL ORDER A dignified G & T.

53 Kinnerton Street, Belgravia, SW1X 8ED.
☎ *020 7235 1135* ● *Hyde Park Corner tube.*

CRAFT BEER, ALE & CIDER

HARP • 66

JERUSALEM TAVERN • 67

CRAFT BEER CO • 69

CASK • 70

EUSTON TAP • 70

THE BULL • 73

CAMDEN TOWN BREWERY BAR • 74

THE EARL OF ESSEX • 75

THE SOUTHAMPTON ARMS • 77

THE DOVE • 78

HAWKES CIDERY & TAPROOM • 79

BREWDOG • 80

CRATE BREWERY • 83

THE ROYAL OAK • 84

THE CROWN & ANCHOR • 84

HOWLING HOPS • 87

THE RAKE • 88

DRAFT HOUSE • 89

THE WHITE HORSE • 90

CRAFT BEER, ALE & CIDER

Porter, stout, lager, saison, fruit; craft or real, cask or keg, a bottle or
a glass… call it what you want – beer is pretty much just hops, yeast,
malt and water. And cider is more or less fermented apples. But, of course,
they're so much more than their constituent ingredients. And they're at
the heart of what pubs are all about. Before mixology, before pork belly
with kale and confit potatoes, before house wine and alcopops and G&Ts,
there was beer. And it's undergoing a full-on renaissance in London.
In 2009 there were just three breweries within the M25 – at the
last count there about 75, and it's growing all the time. Similarly, artisan
cider producers are springing up around the country and sending their barrels
to grateful Londoners (and there's even one in the city now). The bars and
pubs in this section are the ones that put real ale, craft beer and proper cider
at the forefront of everything they do. The best from local, British and global
brewers, sourced, stored and served with care, respect and even a bit of love.

● HARP

Drink... In the beer-drinker's secret in the sightseers' heart of London.

Many pubs display beer mats above the bar like trophies of past conquests, but few can claim as many as this flower-decked free house just a couple of hundred metres from Trafalgar Square. Its enthusiasm for all things hoppy and appley wins it every award going – and what's more, it serves butcher's bangers in baguettes. A beauty.

ESSENTIAL ORDER Always resplendent on the bar is a beer from West Sussex's Dark Star brewery.

47 Chandos Place, Covent Garden, WC2N 4HS.
☎ *020 7836 0291*
🖥 *www.harpcoventgarden.com*
⊖ *Charing Cross tube.*

● JERUSALEM TAVERN

Drink... in the oldest new pub in the city.

It looks ancient, and in a way it is. There was a Jerusalem Tavern in this area as long ago as the fourteenth century, but this building dates from 1719 and only became a pub in 1996. It's owned by Suffolk brewery St Peter's, and so pours little besides its own products, which is no bad thing.

Inside is a modern Clerkenwell reimagining of a seventeenth-century London inn – dark, atmospheric and kept toasty by a real fire.

ESSENTIAL ORDER Anything from St Peter's – the cream stout is especially tasty on a cold night and goes fantastically with one of the pub's sublime pork pies.

53 Britton Street, Clerkenwell, EC1M 5UQ.

☎ *020 7490 4281* 🖥 *www.stpetersbrewery.co.uk*

🚇 *Farringdon tube.*

● CRAFT BEER CO

Drink... the most adventurous selection of beer in Britain.

Fact: it's impossible to drink anything other than brilliant beer at this Leather Lane jewel. There's a commitment to small, independent British breweries, and foreign brews are imported exclusively. By the bottle are what looks like countless more, although someone has counted, and there are over 400. Such dedication means that it's standing-room-only most nights. If you're used to calming brown British beer, you might be pleasantly startled by the sheer daring of some of the offering – fruity Scandinavian pale ales, malty US barleywines, spicy Belgian farmhouse ales.

ESSENTIAL ORDER The Craft Beer Co IPA is brewed exclusively.

82 Leather Lane, Clerkenwell, EC1N 7TR.
☎ *020 7404 7049*
🖥 *www.thecraftbeerco.com*
⊖ *Farringdon tube.*
Branches at Brixton, Covent Garden, Limehouse, Old Street, St Mary Axe.

brews are always in high demand; the Saint
Petersburg Imperial Stout takes no prisoners.
6 Charlwood Street, Pimlico, SW1V 2EE.
☎ *020 7630 7225*
🖥 *www.caskpubandkitchen.com*
⊖ *Pimlico tube.*

● EUSTON TAP

Drink... in a station bar that's worth missing your train for.

Like sentinels presiding over the planning disaster
that is the modern Euston, the station's original
Victorian parcel offices at the gate still stand beside
a non-stop road. They've now been converted into
mini pubs – the West Lodge and the East Lodge,
both longstanding purveyors of craft beer and
British real ales, and part of a mini chain that pops
up at stations across the country. Their minimal
design isn't worth making a song and dance about,
although stop by in summer and the crowd spreads
merrily on to the pavement well into the night.
ESSENTIAL ORDER A powerful American IPA
from Evil Twin.
190 Euston Road, St Pancras, NW1 2EF.
☎ *020 3137 8837*
🖥 *www.eustontap.com*
⊖ *Euston tube. Branch at Waterloo.*

● CASK

Drink... in a craft beer pioneer.

It's a trailblazer in more ways than one – this
modern and minimal place opened in 2009, just
as the London craft beer revolution was in its
infancy. Plus, it's on a residential street near Pimlico
station, well out of the way of the city's trendy bar
hotspots. Cask is another potential claimant for
the title of 'biggest beer range in the city' – ignore
the slightly student-union look of the place and
focus instead on the wondrous selection.

● THE BULL

**Drink... in a Highgate brewpub
that stands out from the herd.**

At first glance, the Bull would appear
to be just another smart north London
gastropub, with tasteful paintwork,
a log fire and a kitchen through a big,
open hatch. But look closer, and there's
practically a field's-worth of hop flowers
hanging from the ceiling, and behind
the bar you might glimpse the gleaming
tanks and pipes of the London Brewing
Company's set-up: following a growing
trend in London, it makes a small range
of beer, sold exclusively here. The Bull
is owned by Dan Fox, who ran the
acclaimed White Horse (see p90) for
years; his thoughtful choice of beer
is the most exceptional this far north
in London.

ESSENTIAL ORDER The flagship Beer
Street is a classic best bitter, and
a great place to start.

13 North Hill, Highgate, N6 4AB.
☎ *020 8341 0510*
🖥 *www.thebullhighgate.co.uk*
⊖ *Highgate tube.*

● CAMDEN TOWN BREWERY BAR

Drink... among the tanks and pipes of Camden's party-starting brewery.

It's the sort of place you hear before you see. Head across the cobbles to the arches underneath Kentish Town West station and the growing chatter suggests something's brewing, and it's not just in the enormous steel vats of one of London's biggest beer producers. Every Thursday, Friday and Saturday Camden Town Brewery opens to drinkers – food stalls provide sustenance, DJs play, and even on winter nights the crowd sprawls from the bar to the covered and heated outdoor tables.

ESSENTIAL ORDER The rich, dry and toasty Camden Ink stout, black as the hands of a Fleet Street printer's devil.

55–59 Wilkin Street Mews, Kentish Town, NW5 3NN.
☎ *020 7485 1671*
🖥 *www.camdentownbrewery.com*
⊖ *Kentish Town West Overground.*

● THE EARL OF ESSEX

Drink... in a perfect pub with a noble heritage.
Far from the crowds of Islington's main
(and mainstream) drinking thoroughfare,
Upper Street, is a sight to cheer: on the wall of
the Earl, a prominently displayed wooden board
advertising the twenty choices on tap in this
handsome house. Visit two days in a row and
it'll look completely different – the menu changes
all the time. What's more, the onsite microbrewery
makes everything from hoppy pale ales to English
best bitters. A smart garden through the back
provides this blue-blood boozer with an extra
dimension in the summer months.
ESSENTIAL ORDER Check the Earl's Twitter
for a photo of the beer of the day.
25 Danbury Street, Islington, N1 8LE.
☎ *020 7424 5828*
💻 *www.earlofessex.net*
θ *Angel tube.*

● THE SOUTHAMPTON ARMS

Drink... in London's original ale and cider house.
When it reopened in 2010, the Southampton Arms
seemed to represent something new: minimal
decor, no fancy name, no flock wallpaper or ironic
taxidermy, no kitchen... But really, it's the spirit
of the pub reborn for the twenty-first century.
Furniture is mainly restricted to penitential pews,
and the town-gas-style lamps look somewhat strict,
but a happy hubbub of customers warms things
up. The resident dog (a girl called Fred) sometimes
makes appearances, which is one reason among
many you should too.

ESSENTIAL ORDER A pint of mild next to the
coal fire (a flat cap wouldn't go amiss either).
139 Highgate Road, Kentish Town, NW5 1LE.
💻 *www.thesouthamptonarms.co.uk*
⊖ *Gospel Oak Overground.*

● THE DOVE

Drink... in a Hackney translation of a Brussels beer bar.

With all the excitement over Britain's burgeoning craft beer scene, it's easy to forget that some nations have been brewing great ale without fuss for centuries, and never stopped. This rambling and rickety old pub has a high number of beers from the Low Countries (more than 100). Team an amber, dark, Trappist, sour or fruit beer with a bowl of moules-frites. (If you're in central London, sister pub the Dovetail is in Clerkenwell.)

ESSENTIAL ORDER The oak-aged Rodenbach Grand Cru is as complex and characterful as a vintage wine.

24–28 Broadway Market,
London Fields, E8 4QJ.
☎ *020 7275 7617*
🖥 *www.dovepubs.com*
⊖ *London Fields rail.*

● HAWKES CIDERY & TAPROOM

Drink... in the cider revolution.

Holding its own with ease in the sea of malt and hops that is Bermondsey's 'Beer Mile' is this pioneering place – London's only city-centre cidery, which aims to give cider the same status that beer currently enjoys. Hawke's started making its Urban Orchard cider in 2014 using apples donated from across London, and today makes a range of craft ciders from different apples to showcase the complexity and range of this newly appreciated category. If drinking the stuff isn't enough, you can stop by for a guided tour, cider-making workshop or just one of the tasty stone-baked pizzas.

ESSENTIAL ORDER Urban Orchard, the cider that started it all – 4.5%, medium-dry and crisp, with a refreshing aftertaste of local collaboration.

92 & 96 Druid Street, Bermondsey, SE1 2HQ.
☎ *020 3903 8387*
🖳 *www.wearehawkes.com/cidery-and-taproom*
⊖ *Bermondsey tube.*

● BREWDOG

Drink... with the upstart insurgents of the brewing world.

In 2006, the Aberdeenshire-based Brewdog set out to shake up the beer industry with its hop-heavy American-style creations and in-your-face marketing. This busy London bar (one of three) follows the same ethos: it's boisterous, brash and stocked with uncompromisingly flavoursome brews. The supposedly 'secret' basement (hint: it's down the stairs) serves beer cocktails and is soundtracked by suitably attitude-heavy bands.

ESSENTIAL ORDER The assertively hoppy Punk IPA is a good place to start.

51-55 Bethnal Green Road, Shoreditch, E1 6LA.
🖥 *www.brewdog.com/bars/shoreditch*
⊖ *Shoreditch High Street Overground.*
Branches throughout London.

● CRATE BREWERY

Drink... a hop, skip and jump from the Olympic Park.

Just across the canal from the site of the Games in the largely industrial Hackney Wick, this craft brewery and pizzeria opened in summer 2012 in a former workshop. It's decked out with found objects – reclaimed wood, lightshades made of old springs – and the result is one of the coolest-looking bars in London, aided by its out-of-the-way location, live jazz and DIY ideology. When it's warm, the canalside seating becomes an urban idyll, with large-scale street art, families of ducks and narrowboats pootling past. The beer is cracking, the pizzas crisp; you'll feel properly in the know when you find this place.

ESSENTIAL ORDER All Crate brews are great, whether lager, bitter, pale ale or stout.

Unit 7, Queen's Yard,
Hackney Wick, E9 5EN.
☎ *020 8533 3331*
🖳 *www.cratebrewery.com*
⊖ *Hackney Wick Overground.*

ESSENTIAL ORDER The Oak is a London tap for much-cherished Sussex brewery Harvey's. Mild, best, IPA, seasonal specials: all are tip-top.
44 Tabard Street, Borough, SE1 4JU.
☎ *020 7357 7173*
🖥 *www.royaloaklondon.co.uk*
⊖ *Borough tube.*

● THE CROWN & ANCHOR

Drink... in a beacon for Brixton beer-buffs.
One of the most profusely stocked, friendliest and all-round most noteworthy pubs in south London, and a real haven for hopheads in an otherwise dry bit of town. On the luxuriously lengthy bar is a luxurious twenty-five taps of ales, ciders and keg craft beer from the likes of Brewdog, Redwell and Windsor & Eton. The stripped-back, unadorned-brick interior is surprisingly cosy, the staff seem to know exactly what you want to drink, and on dark nights, the big Brooklyn Brewery neon on the wall is like a beacon in a stormy sea.
ESSENTIAL ORDER Brixton Brewery is just up the road – there's no finer place to sample its wares. Keep things proudly local with the amber-coloured Effra Ale.
246 Brixton Road, Stockwell, SW9 6AQ.
☎ *020 7737 0060*
🖥 *www.crownandanchorbrixton.co.uk*
⊖ *Brixton tube.*

● THE ROYAL OAK

Drink... here when modern life overwhelms.
On a peaceful street in Borough is a timewarp: step through the doors of the Royal Oak into an era when the pub was a reassuring extension of your living room. There are leave-me-alone stools at the bar for solitary drinkers, there's a mini jumble sale on the mantelpiece, and around the carved wood central island hang what look like granny's decorative plates. Net curtains, rugs on the bare floorboards and squashy sofas complete the picture. A real one-off.

● HOWLING HOPS

Drink... straight from the source.

Howling Hops started as the very cramped in-house brewery of the Cock Tavern in Hackney Central, before a major expansion led to this ex-industrial workshop by the Olympic Park. But the bar here's no tacked-on afterthought: its ten enormous serving tanks in gleaming steel are an inspiring sight and mean that beer really doesn't come any fresher. It's like a modern beer hall, with long communal tables and often a riotously fun atmosphere, and the rough-round-the-edges look make it an easy place to spend an afternoon. Combine a trip here with a visit to the next-door Crate (see p83) for a Hackney Wick mini-brewery crawl.

ESSENTIAL ORDER Close your eyes and point at one of the shiny tanks (although the special-edition IPAs are reliably amazing).

Queens Yard, White Post Lane, Hackney Wick, E9 5EN.
☎ *020 3583 8262* 🖥 *www.howlinghops.co.uk*
⊖ *Hackney Wick Overground.*

● THE RAKE

Drink... in the greatest small bar in London bar none.

A tiny room is dotted with simple tables and chairs, a counter is cramped by a few beer taps, there's a basic heated outdoor area. Plasterboard walls are scrawled with messages from visiting brewers, all singing the praises of this no-nonsense bar; into its minimal space it crams one of London's most exciting beer selections. There are a few decent places to drink around Borough Market; all get packed on trading days, but the Rake is worth the squeeze. If you ever find yourself in Westfield Stratford in need of refreshment, search out sister pub Tap East, which is a grand reason to visit London's biggest shopping centre.

ESSENTIAL ORDER 'No crap on tap,' a sign proclaims – tell the staff what kind of beer you like and you'll be well rewarded.

14a Winchester Walk, Borough, SE1 9AG.
☎ *020 7407 0557* 🖥 *www.utobeer.co.uk*
⊖ *London Bridge tube.*

● DRAFT HOUSE

Drink... in a eight-strong chain of bars that champions all that's brilliant about beer.

'Where the beer flows like wine,' says a sign on the wall at this 'modernised public house', and it's more than just a play on words. Along with its other locations, Draft House aims to treat the product of the grain with as much reverence as has traditionally been afforded to that of the grape. This Clapham branch should be your first choice on a street replete with bars; the others all have the knack of popping up in places that you'll be jolly pleased to find a great pub. Draft House's food, especially the aged Angus burgers, comes recommended too.

ESSENTIAL ORDER There's a 'cask of the day' sold at a very fair price, and it's often sensational.
94 Northcote Road, Clapham, SW11 6QW.
☎ *020 7924 1814* 🖳 *www.drafthouse.co.uk*
⊖ *Clapham Junction Overground.*
Branches at Battersea, Bermondsey, Bethnal Green, Blackfriars, Camden, Fitzrovia, Hammersmith, Monument, Shoreditch, Tower Bridge.

● **THE WHITE HORSE**

**Drink... in west London's beer
and cider frontrunner.**
Enter this airy parkside corner site, and
before you notice the copper-coloured
Pilsner Urquell tanks, the nut-brown
armchairs, the padded pews or the
almost colonial proportions of the
stately room, you'll see the bar. It comes
with more taps than a Bruce Forsyth
routine, and features traditional British
bitters, high-strength monk-brewed
Belgians, and unusual examples like
Italian IPA. Real beer connoisseurs turn
up for festivals celebrating American,
European or local brews, but the rest
of us can dip into the list knowing
we're in safe hands.
ESSENTIAL ORDER If you're not
drinking beer here, you're not
really drinking.
1-3 Parson's Green, Fulham, SW6 4UL.
☎ *020 7736 2115*
🖥 *www.whitehorsesw6.com*
⊖ *Parson's Green tube.*

LIQUID HISTORY

THE FRENCH HOUSE • 96

YE OLDE CHESHIRE CHEESE • 98

RULES • 99

BEAUFORT BAR AND
THE AMERICAN BAR AT THE SAVOY • 101

THE PRINCESS LOUISE • 102

AMERICAN BAR AT THE STAFFORD • 105

DUKE'S • 106

THE BLACK FRIAR • 107

YE OLDE MITRE • 109

JAMAICA WINE HOUSE • 110

THE HOLLY BUSH • 111

BOOKING OFFICE • 112

THE PROSPECT OF WHITBY • 114

THE GEORGE INN • 115

THE BAR AT THE GORING • 116

THE DOVE • 118

THE PRINCE ALFRED • 119

LIQUID HISTORY

The history of London's bars and pubs is the history of London itself. From wine-sipping Romans in their tavernae through Saxons with mead and ale to the gin-crazed Georgians and the porter-swilling Victorians, social changes can be measured by how the city's inhabitants drank. And nowadays, one of its unique selling points is the history bound up in its licensed establishments. Visitors can't get enough of the back stories: truly ancient boozers like Ye Olde Cheshire Cheese in Fleet Street or Ye Olde Mitre in Holborn provide a glimpse into a lost London a world away from the typical tourist zones of the West End. And it's just as important to permanent residents too – places like the George Inn or Rules are a connection to the centuries of Londoners who lived here before. Some of our historical pubs have remained largely unchanged since they were built (the Princess Louise, for example) and with others it's not the building but the biography that deserves a closer look – the French House was home to a whole generation of poets, writers and actors in boho '60s Soho, and the Black Friar is London's only extant art nouveau pub.

● THE FRENCH HOUSE

**Drink... in a corner of England
that is for ever a foreign land.**
Soho was once London's most licentious
locale, an anything-goes playground
where artists, sailors, novelists, free
spirits and foreigners could forget
for a while they were in the capital of
buttoned-up Britain. Those days are
largely gone, but the French House
stands as a bastion of independence and
joie de vivre. During WWII, the French
Resistance under Charles de Gaulle met
here, inspiring its Gallic name; today,
ask for a pint and you'll be offered a half
only; mobiles are banned; monochrome
pictures of former regulars pack the
wood-panelled walls; and the two small
bars resound with spirited merriment.
ESSENTIAL ORDER Find something
(anything) to celebrate, drown your
troubles with bubbles and get tipsy in
the style of a true libertine.
49 Dean Street, Soho, W1D 5BG.
☎ *020 7437 2477 / 2799*
🖥 *www.frenchhousesoho.com*
⊖ *Leicester Square tube.*

● YE OLDE CHESHIRE CHEESE

Drink... and get lost in the mists of time or in the maze of rooms.

The prefix 'Ye Olde' is open to licence, but this certainly is one extra-mature cheese. 'Rebuilt in 1667,' says the sign – after the Great Fire of London – and it looks like it's barely changed since. As such, its dim and atmospheric stone-and-wood bars and dungeon-like cellars are a huge draw for out-of-towners. It's an ancient relic they can actually sit and drink in. When a pub's been around this long it's bound to have attracted its fair share of famous Londoners; the patrons supposed to have tipped a glass here include Dickens, Yeats, Tennyson and, when the Cheese was less Olde, Dr Samuel Johnson.

ESSENTIAL ORDER In the absence of a Pepysian jug of wine, try the closest thing to the traditional smog-thick 'London particular' stout, a bottle of Taddy Porter.

145 Fleet Street, City, EC4A 2BU.
☎ *020 7353 6170* ● *Chancery Lane tube.*

● RULES

Drink... in the oldest restaurant in London.
Opened in 1798, the ground-floor dining room packs them in with its tales of notable historical patrons and its sumptuous English fare; upstairs, the cocktail bar is something of a secret in the area, and although it's a relatively more modern addition, it shares the wonderful sense of antiquity. The design is grandly OTT – like an eccentric laird's Highland hunting lodge, with leaded windows, a moulded mermaid with stag antlers, real fur decorations come Christmas and acres of gilt and mirrors – but the premium spirits and expertly mixed drinks make Rules far too good to leave to the tourists or the traditionalists.

ESSENTIAL ORDER The Rules Cocktail is made with gin, Dubonnet, bitters and sparkling wine.
34–35 Maiden Lane, Covent Garden, WC2E 7LB.
☎ *020 7836 5314* 💻 *www.rules.co.uk*
⊖ *Covent Garden tube.*

● THE BEAUFORT BAR AND THE AMERICAN BAR AT THE SAVOY

Drink... in the world-class bars of a world-famous hotel.

Both bars in the iconic Savoy could hold a claim to being the most refined in London. Following an epic refurbishment in 2010, they reopened with two distinct but equally glamorous personalities. Past the Thames Foyer, the Beaufort is dusky, sexy, opulent and clad seductively in black and gold; the more famous American Bar, perhaps one for afternoons rather than evenings, was a birthplace of the modern cocktail and is dapper, discreet and soundtracked by a grand piano. Can there be more striking backdrops in London for the taking of drinks?

ESSENTIAL ORDER In the Beaufort, there are 25 champagnes by the glass. In the American, it has to be a classic; head barman Harry Craddock created the White Lady here in the 1920s.

Strand, WC2R 0EU.

☎ *020 7836 4343*

🖥 *www.fairmont.com/savoy-london*

⊖ *Charing Cross tube.*

● THE PRINCESS LOUISE

Drink... in a grand old London gin palace.

Once upon a time, all pubs were like this. Or, at least, pubs like this would have been less uncommon. The Princess Louise survives as a wonderful example of the late nineteenth-century 'gin palace', designed with maximum extravagance to instill in Londoners a sense that for as long as it took to drink a pint, they were lord of the manor. Take in the mirrors, the etched glass, the gold-leaf pillars, the wooden partitions, and say to yourself: they don't make them like this any more.

ESSENTIAL ORDER The pub's now under the ownership of the Samuel Smith Brewery, and its hefty and bittersweet Oatmeal Stout is the pick of the bunch.

208 High Holborn, Holborn, WC1V 7EP.
☎ *020 7405 8816*
⊖ *Holborn tube.*

● AMERICAN BAR AT THE STAFFORD

Drink... in an Ivy League clubhouse.
Most Londoners think they have no have reason to venture into the cobbled and gaslit streets of St James's, let alone venture further still into this exclusive hotel. But don't let the guests have it to themselves – it has one of the only two American bars left in London (they were popular in the 1930s), and it's a unique place. The walls and ceiling are liberally bedecked with US memorabilia donated by visitors over the years, including pennants, baseball caps, football helmets, signed photos. The days of gentlemen being forced to wear a jacket and tie in the bar may have gone, but a pleasing old-school sensibility remains.
ESSENTIAL ORDER It has to be an American classic – the Manhattan is done particularly well, as you'd hope.
The Stafford, St James's Place,
St James's, SW1A 1NJ.
☎ 020 7493 0111
● *Green Park tube.*

● DUKE'S

Drink... in James Bond's bar of choice.
You could order a classic cocktail. You could go for champagne (Pol Roger Cuvée Sir Winston Churchill seems right), or an aged calvados. But there's one drink Duke's is famous for. Ask for a martini, and as you sit in a Downton Abbey armchair under historical portraits of stern members of the landed classes, a white-jacketed barman wheels over a trolley of chilled spirits and exquisite glassware, and proceeds to concoct the cocktail. It's a superb piece of tableside theatre and one of London's quintessential experiences, made more significant when you learn it was Duke's that inspired author Ian Fleming to make his 007 a Martini man. The full Bond tux isn't necessary, but it's vital to make an effort with your attire.
ESSENTIAL ORDER The Vesper: London gin, Polish vodka, Lillet vermouth, bitters and orange oil. *St James's Place, St James's, SW1A 1NY.* ☎ *020 7491 4840* 🖥 *www.dukeshotel.com* ⊖ *Green Park tube.*

● THE BLACK FRIAR

Drink... in an art nouveau City sanctuary.

Don't wait till you get to the end of your pint before tipping your head back in this one-of-a-kind arts-and-craft masterpiece. In friezes around the ceiling, merrie monks carouse and converse in relief, their good humour tempered somewhat by the ascetic decrees carved adjacent ('finery is foolery', for example).

ESSENTIAL ORDER Take in the arched fireplace alcove and the churchly architectural detailing and wonder at why it took a campaign from John Betjeman to save this pub from demolition in the 1960s. Then drink to its blessed continued existence.

174 Queen Victoria Street, City, EC4V 4EG.
☎ *020 7236 5474*
⊖ *Blackfriars tube.*

● YE OLDE MITRE

Drink... in a Cambridgeshire criminal's hideaway.

At one time this pub existed on land owned by the Bishop of Ely, a town in Cambridgeshire. His palace was nearby, and the story goes that felons on the run used to be able to claim refuge from City of London constabulary here. Probably best not to test that theory out, however. The Mitre was originally built in 1546, although rebuilt in 1782 and refitted inside in 1930, so its colourful history isn't immediately obvious. It's also notoriously hard to find; follow the hum of animated conversation down an alley from Hatton Garden to a cosy and characterful hideaway.

ESSENTIAL ORDER Real ales are a strong point, and the Scottish Deuchar's is usually pouring.

1 Ely Place, Holborn, EC1N 6SJ.
☎ *020 7405 4751*
🖥 *www.yeoldemitreholborn.co.uk*
⊖ *Chancery Lane tube.*

● JAMAICA WINE HOUSE

Drink... in an unofficial City boardroom.
On the site of this properly hidden-away City stalwart stood London's first coffee house, 'at the sign of Pasqua Rosee's Head', built in 1652 to provide a meeting place for industrious merchants. The Jamaica Wine House is now a traditional pub a world away from the big and brash chain bars that dominate the Square Mile, and it's as good for ales as it is for its titular refreshment. It's in taverns like this – reached through a maze of ancient alleyways, and with dark wood partitions – that business has been done the old-fashioned way for centuries, with a handshake, a nod and a pint.

ESSENTIAL ORDER Celebrate closing a deal (or pretend you just did) with something rich and red. *St Michael's Alley, Cornhill, City, EC3V 9DS.*
☎ *020 7929 6972*
🖥 *www.jamaicawinehouse.co.uk*
⊖ *Bank tube.*

● THE HOLLY BUSH

Drink... at the top of a Hampstead hill.

Of all the perfectly lovely pubs in perfectly lovely Hampstead village, the Holly Bush is the most perfect. Climb through steep and winding lanes away from the post-Heath-strolling throng and you'll be rewarded by a warren of tobacco-coloured rooms and a few Fuller's beers; the Holly Bush has been an inn since 1800 and looks every year of it, in the nicest possible way (although the building itself is older).

Combine a stop-off here with a trip to the nearby seventeenth-century merchant's dwelling Fenton House. Plus, a quick fact with which to bore your drinking pals: the whole London Underground network is at its deepest point below the Holly Bush: 68.8m.

ESSENTIAL ORDER A special bottle of Fuller's Vintage. An old, old ale in an old, old pub.

22 Holly Mount, Hampstead, NW3 6SG.
☎ *020 7435 2892*
🖳 *www.hollybushhampstead.co.uk*
⊖ *Hampstead tube.*

● BOOKING OFFICE

Drink... in a Victorian cathedral of cocktails.

Housed in the former ticket office of St Pancras station and now part of the magnificent Renaissance hotel, this all-day bar and restaurant is surely one of the most impressive places to drink in London. At ground level is a sweeping marble bar, but look up and you won't fail to be awed: architect Sir George Gilbert Scott's gothic room soars with ecclesiastical arches, buttresses and leaded windows. The Victorians built pretty special pubs, but their stations were something else.

ESSENTIAL ORDER A revived classic from the 1800s: the Soyer au Champagne is made with cider brandy, cherry liqueur, vanilla ice cream and champagne.

St Pancras Renaissance, Euston Road, King's Cross, NW1 2AR.
☎ *020 7841 3566*
🖥 *www.stpancraslondon.com*
⊖ *King's Cross tube.*

● THE PROSPECT OF WHITBY

Drink... in a Dickensian dockers' tavern right on the river.

The nautical history is laid on thick and unapologetically in this Wapping watering hole, reaching its peak with the modern addition of a noose on the foreshore: this was a site of piratical hangings in bygone days. 'Dating back to 1520', the pub claims – well, the flagstone floor does, at least, but even still the rest of it is sufficiently aged to give visitors a good idea of what this atmospheric area must have been like when the docks were working. Take a drink out to the terrace on a cold night and gaze out over the dark river to the wharves of Rotherhithe and the twinkling towers of Canary Wharf.

ESSENTIAL ORDER A hearty glass of grog will make the seafaring scene come to life.

57 Wapping Wall, Wapping, E1W 3SH.
☎ *020 7481 1095*
⊖ *Wapping Overground.*

● THE GEORGE INN

Drink... in London's last galleried coaching inn.

This pub down a lane off Borough High Street was rebuilt in 1686, and it remains a piece of living history; it was once a stop-off for travellers making their way into the City, and has retained its balustraded galleries along the front of the building. But it's no dusty artefact. In summer, the cobbled courtyard is a magnet for workers from the surrounding and incongruously modern offices, and inside it's suitably timeworn too: the Parliament Bar, with its serving hatch, is an evocative spot.

For the full and fascinating history, see Pete Brown's excellent book 'Shakespeare's Local'.

ESSENTIAL ORDER Take a drink outside and look up at the Shard – 300 years of London architecture in one glance.

75–77 Borough High Street, Borough, SE1 1NH.
☎ 020 7407 2056 ▭ www.george-southwark.co.uk
⊖ London Bridge tube.

● THE BAR AT THE GORING

Drink... in the royals' favourite bar.
There are exquisite hotels aplenty in London, but few have the sense of refinement of The Goring, built in 1910 and owned by the same family since. The bar is an Edwardian haven of deep-red walls and old-school manners; drinks aren't cutting edge, although they are expertly made. Prices are high, naturally, but look at the richness of the surroundings, the courtly service and the extras like canapés in the evening and nibbles on all tables. House rules stipulate that mobiles may not be used, even when the Queen's staff have their Christmas party here. It's that sort of place.

ESSENTIAL ORDER There's half-a-million pounds-worth of wine in the cellars: it would be a shame not to try some.

The Goring, 15 Beeston Place, Belgravia, SW1W 0JW.
☎ *020 7396 9000*
🖥 *www.thegoring.com*
⊖ *Victoria tube.*

● **THE DOVE**

Drink... in the world's smallest bar room.

On a sunny day, the whole of Hammersmith knows that the riverside terrace at the Dove is one of the city's most desirable. The problem with that: it's tiny, as is the rest of the centuries-old pub. So arrive early if you want to bag a prime seat overlooking a languid curve of the Thames to watch the rowers power past. Or skip the sunny season and visit in winter, when the real fire turns the flagstoned front room into one of the cosiest retreats in west London. And, keep an eye out for the hidden entrance to the tiny secret cubbyhole...

ESSENTIAL ORDER Fuller's Griffin Brewery is about half a mile upriver. On a cold day go for the London Porter, black as the midnight Thames.

19 Upper Mall, Hammersmith, W6 9TA.
☎ *020 8748 9474*
🖥 *www.dovehammersmith.co.uk*
⊖ *Hammersmith tube.*

● THE PRINCE ALFRED

Drink... in the most divisive pub in the capital.

The Victorians were a funny bunch. They built the most spectacular temples dedicated to drinking, but went out of their way to ensure that different social classes never clapped eyes on one another while patronising them. This beautifully preserved boozer not far from the canals of Little Venice has some of the most notable mid-nineteenth-century pub features left in London: 'snob' screens and partitioned snugs, originally with their own entrances to the street, shielded men from women, proles from respectable sorts, and all manner of nefarious activity from the landlord. An architectural historian's dream, and a very decent pub for the casual appreciator.

ESSENTIAL ORDER Whatever you like. No one can see you.

5a Formosa Street, Maida Vale, W9 1EE.
☎ *020 7286 3287*
🖥 *www.theprincealfred.com*
⊖ *Warwick Avenue tube.*

WINE AND SPIRIT SPECIALISTS

TERROIRS • 124

BAR TERMINI • 124

VINOTECA • 127

BLACK ROCK • 128

SHOCHU LOUNGE • 130

ARTESIAN • 131

7 TALES • 132

BOISDALE • 135

JOSÉ • 135

THE SUN TAVERN • 136

LOUNGE BOHEMIA • 137

SAGER + WILDE • 138

RUM KITCHEN • 138

PORTOBELLO STAR • 141

KENSINGTON WINE ROOMS • 142

WINE AND SPIRIT SPECIALISTS

Some occasions call for something other than a pint of beer.
A refreshing gin and tonic on a hot summer evening, a warming
brandy on a frosty night, a glass of something white and vivacious
(or red and fruity), a sweet, salty, smoky or peaty malt whisky... All the
bars in this chapter are noted for their commitment to the grape and the
grain, whether it's the hundreds of varieties of Scotch in Boisdale,
the natural wines in Terroirs, or the shrine to high-class
rum that is Artesian. And it's a good time to be a specialist in spirits.
Following a fallow few decades, there are several enthusiastic producers
making small-batch gin in London again, from Highgate's Sacred to
the gingery, citrussy Little Bird; around the city, discerning drinkers are
recognising the merits of mezcal, sipping tequilas, barrel-aged rums and
sherries. More unconventional spirits are entering the mainstream too
– pisco, shochu, soju, Japanese whisky. And London is a wine-drinker's
paradise: the city's auctioneers break records with the world's most
expensive bottles of wine, but its bars are accessible to all.

average bottle of supermarket plonk – emphatic, often wildly unfettered flavours ('farmy' is one complimentary description used). You don't have to eat here, but the small plates, charcuterie and cheese are excellent partners to the wines.
ESSENTIAL ORDER The earthy, dark-fruited Vino di Anna 'Jeudi 15' is typical of the natural winemaking technique.
5 William IV Street, Covent Garden, WC2N 4DW.
☎ *020 7036 0660 ⌨ www.terroirswinebar.com*
⊖ *Charing Cross tube.*

● BAR TERMINI

Drink... in a train station waiting room straight from a Fellini film.
By day, this tiny Italian bar does a fine line in super-strong espressos. Come evening, the lights dim and it segues into a suave spot for the taking of cocktails, and the speciality here is the Negroni: gin, Campari and vermouth (mixed and chilled so it doesn't need to be served over ice). There are a few other cocktails on the menu – sophisticated and assured – all served by bow-tie-sporting staff. But no one does those bitter, grown-up, satisfying aperitivi like the Italians, and no one in London does them like Bar Termini.
ESSENTIAL ORDER The Negroni, served in an elegant little custom-made glass: perfect every time.
7 Old Compton Street, Soho, W1D 5JE.
☎ *07860 945018 ⌨ www.bar-termini.com*
⊖ *Tottenham Court Road tube. Branch at Marylebone.*

● TERROIRS

Drink... a delicious glass of white, red, rosé or orange.
Yes, orange wine does exist (it's basically white grapes macerated in the red wine style), and it's a style all of its own. Terroirs is one of the best places in London to try natural and biodynamic wines, which are made by fanatical small-scale viticulturalists, in tune with the seasons, unfiltered, unsulphured and using strict organic methods. The results are very unlike your

● VINOTECA

Drink... in a democratic wine bar that could make oenophiles of us all.
There are few wine bars in London that put so much thought and care into their offering, with a list running to hundreds of bottles, all chosen from exciting producers. It's also affordable — there are 25 by the glass (kept fresh in an Enomatic preservation machine), and prices start at under £4. Excellent cheese and charcuterie keeps the peckish satisfied, but Vinoteca is also a splendid restaurant in its own right.
ESSENTIAL ORDER For a discreet little treat, there's prosecco on tap. Hard to say no to that.
53–55 Beak Street, Soho, W1F 9SH.
☎ *020 3544 7411*
💻 *www.vinoteca.co.uk*
⊖ *Piccadilly Circus tube.*
Branches at Chiswick, Farringdon, King's Cross, Marylebone.

● BLACK ROCK

Drink… straight from the table.
Through the darkness in this miniature basement whisk(e)y bar, you'll be able to make out a long wooden table running the length of the room. It's formed from a single ancient oak tree, and it has two covered channels cut into it, lined with wooden staves; they're used to age two house whisky blends, which are dispensed from taps at the end. Down one wall is a row of cabinets containing the incredible collection of bottles, which will have aficionados excited for sure, but the helpful taste-led classification (and democratic pricing) means everyone will be a convert by the time they leave.

ESSENTIAL ORDER A snifter of the American Wood – house-blend whisky with morello cherries.
9 Christopher Street, Shoreditch, EC2A 2BS.
☎ *020 7247 4580*
🖥 *www.blackrock.bar*
⊖ *Liverpool Street tube.*

BLACK ROCK

BY THE DRAM

LIMOUSIN WOOD (35ml) 6
Bulleit bourbon, mint, sugar, bitters

AMERICAN WOOD (35ml) 6
Table whisky blend, cherry memories

LIBRARY
(35ml)
(35ml) 7
(35ml) 9
(35ml) 11
(35ml) POA

HIGHBALLS

BALANCE
Bowmore, Islay mineral water, Islay ice

FRUIT 8
Black Label, cherry river, clear oj, Islay ice

SPICE
Kavalan, sherry, pomelo, schezuan liquer

SMOKE 12
Nikka, ginger, yuzushu soda, Caol Ila

FRAGRANCE 11
Cardhu, absinthe, creme brulee soda

SWEET 10
Bulleit rye, house ginger ale, lime spritz

COCHTAILS

BALANCE 9
Haig Clubman, Tanqueray 10, Lillet, peat

FRUIT 9
Roe & Co, pineapple drop, nettle, Drambuie

SPICE 10
Singleton, Cocchi barolo chinato, Drambuie

SMOKE 9
Lagavulin 8, Fernet coffee distilate, speculoos

FRAGRANCE 11
Dalwhinnie, violette, lavender oil, citric

SWEET 10
Bulleit, falernum, oleo saccharum, bitters

BEER

DOG IPA
WN PILSNER 6
WHITE ALE 6
LTIC STOUT 6

SCRAN

RAW OYSTERS (EACH) 9
Helford River, Storm air

BAHED OYSTERS (EACH) 2.5
Gratinee, garlic, beer crumb

VEGGIE HAGGIS BALLS 3
Sherry salsa

SCOTCH EGG
Peated hollandaise

● SHOCHU LOUNGE

Drink... Japan's favourite spirit.

Everyone's heard of sake, and it's well known that the Japanese venerate whisky too, but actually the country's most-supped alcoholic drink after beer is shochu, still fairly rare in the West. It's distilled from various bases including grains, sweet potatoes and vegetables, each giving it a different character; fruits and herbs are used as infusions too. In this sleek, metropolitan underground bar it's served neat over hand-carved blocks of ice or shaken into sophisticated cocktails with Eastern additions like yuzu, green tea and rosewater.

ESSENTIAL ORDER A plum ume shu – straight – to acquaint yourself with this delicate spirit.

37 Charlotte Street, Fitzrovia, W1T 1RR.
☎ *020 7580 6464*
🖥 *www.rokarestaurant.com*
⊖ *Goodge Street tube.*

● ARTESIAN

Drink... at a five-star bar that almost didn't exist.

It's hard to believe when you survey the monumental edifice of the grand Langham hotel, or marvel at the marble and towering columns in its sumptuous bar, but over its 150-year history it was damaged by aerial bombing, commandeered by the BBC and survived a 1980 proposal to demolish. It now serves as the ideal high-class haven for footsore shoppers from Oxford Street. The cocktails are rightly lauded (although some are presented with what is more tableside pantomime than theatre), but rum is a speciality, and the lavish and grandiose room is a great place for an afternoon glass of wine too.

ESSENTIAL ORDER One of the many superior sipping rums, like Brugal Extra Viego from the Dominican Republic: spicy, nutty and treacly as a Christmas cake.

1C Portland Place, Marylebone, W1B 1JA.
☎ *020 7636 1000*
🖳 *www.artesian-bar.co.uk*
⊖ *Oxford Circus tube.*

● 7 TALES

Drink... in an underground izakaya.
There's the Tokyo of the imagination, and then there's the real Tokyo – to experience a bit of the former with none of the crowding or 14-hour work days, this dark and laidback little cocktail grotto underneath chef Jason Atherton's Sosharu restaurant is your portal. The cocktails are classics with a creative Japanese twist – Turnmills Rice Wine is a martini with sushi rice-washed gin – the izakaya bar snacks are perfect with a Hitachino Nest craft beer, and the list of Japanese whiskies is impressive.
ESSENTIAL ORDER If you've never properly sampled a proper sake, the bartenders here will set you on the right track.
64 Turnmill Street, Farringdon, EC1M 5RR.
☎ *020 3805 2304*
🖥 *www.sosharulondon.com/ seventales-board*
⊖ *Farringdon tube.*

● BOISDALE

Drink... in a Highland castle on the Isle of Dogs.
It's an understatement to say there's whisky galore at this eastern branch of the three-strong Boisdale group. The vast space is a feast of Caledoniana, with yards of tartan, stuffed game trophies and stately leather armchairs, and one of London's few cigar terraces. Perch at the counter in front of the magnificent 12-metre display of bottles and allow the whisky-encyclopedia of a barman to talk you through your choices. There's something from just about every Scottish distillery, silent and operational, as well as rare and limited-edition expressions. It gets pricey – over £600 for a Black Bowmore 1964 Sherry Cask – but there's something for all pockets as well as palates.

ESSENTIAL ORDER An exclusive Boisdale bottling – Longmorn or Linkwood from Speyside, Teaninich or Clynelish from the Highlands.
Cabot Place, Canary Wharf, E14 4QT.
☎ *020 7715 5818* 🖥 *www.boisdale.co.uk*
⊖ *Canary Wharf tube.*
Branches at Belgravia, Bishopsgate, Mayfair.

● JOSÉ

Drink... in Andalusia by way of Bermondsey.
London's overcrowded restaurant tables can't cope: they just weren't built to fit the endless succession of 'small plates' that every kitchen now wants to serve. Chef José Pizarro has to take some of the blame for this – when he opened this snug tapas bar on the delightful Bermondsey Street a few years ago, everyone realised how much fun it was to sit at a bar (or more likely stand by a table) with a cold glass of perky sherry and a few snacks – bellota ham, prawns with chilli, or fried goat's cheese with honey. Team them with a few cañas of easygoing Estrella beer, or check out the all-Spanish wine list filled with fun stuff.

ESSENTIAL ORDER A glass of the special aged palo cortado antique from Jerez.
104 Bermondsey Street, Bermondsey, SE1 3UB.
🖥 *www.josepizarro.com/jose-tapas-bar*
⊖ *London Bridge tube.*

● THE SUN TAVERN

Drink... in an East End pub with an Irish soul.
This corner of Bethnal Green is becoming craft beer central, with Mother Kelly's, the King's Arms, Redchurch Brewery and the Sebright Arms leading the way. The Sun Tavern does have a very decent few taps of local craft beers, but it also has another major alcoholic draw – the finest selection of Irish whiskey and poitín in London. Irish whiskey is undergoing a renaissance, with many world-beating varieties made in small-batch distilleries, and its rebellious brother poitín has gone from bathtub moonshine to a legal artisan spirit. It's all served in a dark, polished remix of an old, traditional East End pub.

ESSENTIAL ORDER Can't choose between spirit or beer? A half of a local beer (Redchurch is brilliant) with a whiskey chaser is perfect.
441 Bethnal Green Road, Bethnal Green, E2 0AN.
☎ *020 7739 4097* 🖥 *www.thesuntavern.co.uk*
⊖ *Bethnal Green tube.*

● LOUNGE BOHEMIA

Drink... in a Cold War Eastern Bloc jazz bunker.
You could walk past the anonymous doorway of
this clandestine basement without ever knowing it
was here, and every night thousands of beered-up
City/Shoreditch types do. The website doesn't give
much away either. But here's the intelligence: you
absolutely must book and you won't get in wearing
a suit. When you've passed those tests, you'll find a
diminutive cocktail bar dressed simply

in midcentury furniture which does a great line in
everything Czech – eaux de vie, homemade infused
vodkas, Regent Bohemian lager, borovicka juniper
brandy, Becherovka bitters... Don't overlook the
avant-garde cocktails, though, which are incredible.
ESSENTIAL ORDER The Old Castro – cigar-infused
rum, vanilla candy floss, orange bitters and
a large measure of bar performance.
1e Great Eastern Street, Shoreditch, EC2A 3EJ.
☎ *07720 707000* ▭ *www.loungebohemia.com*
⊖ *Shoreditch High Street Overground.*

● SAGER + WILDE

Drink... wine without the wankiness.

After years working in hospitality – in Europe, London and the US – Michael Sager knew that people who loved great wine didn't always love the sorts of places it was served in. So he opened this initially unassuming little place in Hackney, and every day he and his staff open bottles of interesting, rare, unusual, singular and thoughtfully made wine, often by small producers, many of which are served by the glass. It's an informal and cool little place, like the kind of bar you might find on the last night of your European city break and that you wish you'd walked past earlier; service is always spot-on, and the simple bar snacks make it somewhere you'll want to linger for more than just a glass.

ESSENTIAL ORDER Sit at the bar and ask the staff what their favourite wine is that day.

193 Hackney Road, Hoxton, E2 8JL.

☎ *020 8127 7330* 🖥 *www.sagerandwilde.com*

⊖ *Hoxton Overground. Branch at Bethnal Green.*

● RUM KITCHEN

Drink... in a West Indian beach shack for the west London set.

Despite the driftwood panelling, Rum Kitchen could hardly be called rustic – Prince Harry is among the sort of castaways who wash up here. But it's a lively and always rocking joint, a place to treat rum with reverence or just knock it back in the fantastic cocktails. The dark basement below the restaurant resonates to the sound of reggae and other island vibes, and the barmen know everything there is to know about the spirit of the Caribbean.

ESSENTIAL ORDER Daquiri, Zombie or punch: they're all made with aplomb, although there's a bounty-worth of rums to be sipped and savoured.

6–8 All Saints Road, Notting Hill, W11 1HH.

☎ *020 3668 2538* 🖥 *www.therumkitchen.com*

⊖ *Ladbroke Grove tube. Branches at Brixton, Soho.*

● PORTOBELLO STAR

Drink... in London's only gin museum.
Is there anyone more passionate about
the history, distilling and drinking
possibilities of gin than the founders
of the Star? On the ground floor is a
good-times Notting Hill bar with an
enormous range of gins, vintage spirits
and single-botanical infusions. Upstairs
is the Ginstitute – a space dedicated to
educating the curious imbiber about the
wondrous spirit itself. Book a session,
which can be as serious or as fun as
you like, and you'll leave with your own
bespoke bottle. A ginspirational place.
ESSENTIAL ORDER The house
gin martini, made with Portobello Road
gin, Lillet Blanc vermouth, bitters and a
twist of grapefruit.
171 Portobello Road,
Notting Hill, W11 2DY.
☎ *020 7229 8220*
▭ *www.portobellostarbar.co.uk*
⊖ *Ladbroke Grove tube.*

● KENSINGTON WINE ROOMS

Drink... help-yourself tasters of wines for every inclination.
There are few places in London that take wine so seriously or strive to make drinking it an experience for all to enjoy as this chic bar among the posh antique shops of Kensington Church Street. A swish Enomatic machine keeps 40 bottles fresh and available by the glass, plus there's a neat option to load a card with credit and get sampling. Experts are on hand to dispense advice.
ESSENTIAL ORDER Wines start at around £4 a glass – dive in and start exploring.
127–129 Kensington Church Street, Kensington, W8 7LP.
☎ *020 7727 8142*
🖥 *www.winerooms.london*
⊖ *Notting Hill Gate tube.*
Branches at Fulham, Hammersmith.

WITH A TWIST

MR FOGG'S • 149

BLUE POSTS • 150

THE AULD SHILLELAGH • 151

SCOTTISH STORES • 152

THE PRIDE OF SPITALFIELDS • 154

THE BOOK CLUB • 155

WELL & BUCKET • 157

MAYOR OF SCAREDY CAT TOWN • 158

THE FALTERING FULLBACK • 159

AQUA SHARD • 160

FRANK'S CAFE • 162

THE SHIP • 163

THE LITTLE BAR • 164

THE MAYFLOWER • 165

CABLE CAFE • 167

THE HARWOOD ARMS • 168

TRAILER HAPPINESS • 170

BAD SPORTS • 170

WITH A TWIST

In a city with so many bars and pubs, there are bound to be
a few that break the mould. Those which diverge from the usual
'room in which to drink' model. There are loads of eccentric,
idiosyncratic and downright unusual drinking establishments
in London. But just because a bar has a silly name, or a password
is required to get in, or it's at the top of a tall building, doesn't mean
it's actually worth leaving the house for. The places in this chapter, however,
all have something that set them apart from the masses, and they're more
than deserving of your custom. Some are local pubs, some are high-end
cocktail bars, but all are uncategorisable. They're for special occasions, for
celebrations, for perking up a mundane Monday night, for those times
when you need more than just a pub quiz to keep you entertained.

● MR FOGG'S

Drink... in the souvenir-stuffed home of a Victorian explorer. On paper, it sounds a bit silly – a Phileas Fogg-themed room displaying all manner of artefacts from the fictional gentleman's travels: a hot-air balloon, flags, penny farthings, animal trophies... But underneath this fastidiously observed theme, there's a very good bar. Service is courteous and eager-to-please, the leather seats are generously plush, and the cocktails are expertly made. **ESSENTIAL ORDER** The bracing East India – a mixture of European and tropical constituents – seems apt.
15 Bruton Lane, Mayfair, W1J 6JD.
☎ *020 7036 0608*
🖳 *www.mr-foggs.com*
⊖ *Green Park tube.*

● BLUE POSTS

Drink... in an ancient Soho pub reborn.
In the heart of the West End, proof that
the pub hasn't died quite yet – it just
moves with the times. It's a bit posher
than your standard British boozer, for
sure, with a dining counter, smart wood
and just-so fittings, but there's plenty
of beer on tap and anyone's welcome
to drop by for a pint and a snack (the
better sort of sausage roll, say). Upstairs
there's a cocktail bar, the Mulwray, that's
cosy and still a bit pubby, and a sit-down
restaurant in the basement.
ESSENTIAL ORDER A Thornbridge
Helles with house-made paprika
crackling – lager and scratchings for
twenty-first-century London.
28 Rupert Street, Soho, W1D 6DJ.
🖳 *www.theblueposts.co.uk*
⊖ *Piccadilly Circus tube.*

● THE AULD SHILLELAGH

Drink... in Ireland, in Hackney.

The staff are all Irish, the customers all seem to be Irish, the pennants and pictures on the walls of this narrow Stoke Newington boozer are all Irish. At weekends a live band fiddles and strums away in the corner. There's not much other than Guinness to drink, although enough of it must be sunk here to fill Galway Bay. Among London's many Irish-ish pubs, the Auld Shillelagh stands out as a genuinely foot-tapping, hand-clapping, glass-clinking Emerald Isle gem. It's enough to make you yearn for the old country, even if your experience starts and ends with a 07:35 Ryanair flight to Dublin.

ESSENTIAL ORDER What else but the black stuff, poured perfectly every time.

105 Stoke Newington Church Street,
Stoke Newington, N16 0UD.
☎ *020 7249 5951*
⊖ *Stoke Newington rail.*

● SCOTTISH STORES

Drink... in a railway pub that's so good you might miss your train.

In the not-so-distant past, the Scottish Stores was the Flying Scotsman, a pub within an easy baggage-wheel of King's Cross station, which was famous for its strippers and not much else. Since its inception it was always a bit rough-and-ready, reflecting the transitory and licentious nature of its neighbourhood. But times have changed, and now it's a beautifully restored arts-and-crafts pub with loads of great beer and even a roof terrace, high above the non-stop streets of King's Cross – it may not be bucolic, quite, but after a few hours on a stuffy train from Edinburgh, it's just what you need.

ESSENTIAL ORDER Arrive a bit early for your train, have a quick half from the well-kept range, continue your journey that bit happier.

2–4 Caledonian Road, King's Cross, N1 9DU. ☎ *020 3384 6497*
🖥 *www.thescottishstores.co.uk*
🚇 *King's Cross St Pancras tube.*

● THE PRIDE OF SPITALFIELDS

Drink... in the coolest uncool pub in London.
Most of the bars around Brick Lane have
followed fashion to cater for the hordes of hipsters
who flock to this famous old street nightly –
but not the Pride. With its net curtains, wood-
burning stove, patterned carpet and blood-red
walls, it's a glimpse into an East End largely lost –
but as well as that, it's a friendly, cosy and quirky
place to escape the real world. Youngsters on
nights out rub shoulders with seasoned locals
and elderly fixtures who look like they never
leave the place, while the pub cat surveys it
all disinterestedly.
ESSENTIAL ORDER Something by London
microbrewery Truman's – it was made for
more than 300 years at the Black Eagle Brewery
nearby in Brick Lane.
3 Heneage Street, Whitechapel, E1 5LJ.
☎ *020 7247 8933*
⊖ *Aldgate East tube.*

● THE BOOK CLUB

Drink... in a twenty-first-century social club.

Thankfully a lot more exciting than its name suggests, the Book Club provides all manner of enlightening distraction for Shoreditch in its imaginatively fitted-out space. Both the breakfast-to-late-night food and the party-time drinks are enough to keep anyone off the streets, but check out the extracurricular activities: a packed events timetable includes DJs and bands, craft classes, yoga, quizzes, jumble sales, film nights, talks, life drawing... And a permanent ping pong table even allows for a bit of exercise. There's no bar in London that puts so much effort into keeping its patrons entertained.

ESSENTIAL ORDER Take a group of pals and get stuck in to the jugs of cocktails to share.

100–106 Leonard Street, Shoreditch, EC2A 4RH.
☎ *020 7684 8618*
🖥 *www.wearetbc.com*
⊖ *Old Street tube.*

● WELL & BUCKET

Drink... in a Victorian pub that came back from the dead.

By 2012, the Well & Bucket was a sad sight; the premises had been occupied by a leather goods wholesaler, then closed completely. But in 2013 it reopened for its intended purpose, and revealed a real stunner beneath the years of neglect: original tiles, now restored with a modern macabre twist. It's now busy and buzzing, and craft beer is its speciality, with 18 on draft. In the dark and secretive vaults of the pub's old cellar is the 5CC cocktail club, which would be worthy of an entry in this book on its own.

ESSENTIAL ORDER A Kernel London porter with oysters upstairs; a short and punchy cocktail downstairs.

143 Bethnal Green Road,
Bethnal Green, E2 7DG.
☎ *020 3664 6454*
🖥 *www.wellandbucket.com*
⊖ *Shoreditch High Street Overground.*

● MAYOR OF SCAREDY CAT TOWN

Drink... in a fridge.

Well, to be more accurate, behind a fridge. The chiller in question is a retro American model in Spitalfields diner the Breakfast Club: tell a staff member you're here to see the mayor, and a secret door leads down to what might be the daftest-named bar in London – and maybe the most frolicsome too. In an era of po-faced Prohibition pretenders, it's great to see somewhere take the 'speakeasy' theme with far more than the recommended pinch of salt. The 'house rules' includes an insistence you leave by a different exit to maintain the secrecy.

ESSENTIAL ORDER The classic cocktails are all straightforward but splendid.

12–16 Artillery Lane, Spitalfields, E1 7LS.
☎ *020 7078 9639*
🖥 www.themayorofscaredycattown.com
⊖ Liverpool Street tube.

● THE FALTERING FULLBACK

Drink... in a vertical garden that grows up and up.

This slightly suburban oddity is like three pubs in one. There's a casual front bar hung with all sorts of junk-shop esoterica, and a sports-friendly back room with big screens showing all the football and rugby, but the real draw is the garden. Its footprint is small but it takes to the skies – stacked up are four decked floors, some covered, some open, festooned with flowers, plants and trinkets, all offering numerous opportunities to sit in a vertical horticultural paradise.

ESSENTIAL ORDER A cold Vedett lager amid the greenery is hard to beat come summer.

19 Perth Road, Stroud Green, N4 3HB.
☎ *020 7272 5834*
⌨ *www. falteringfullback.com*
⊖ *Finsbury Park tube.*

● AQUA SHARD

Drink... in some views with your booze.

Few bars match up in height to Aqua Shard, sandwiched halfway up the tallest and pointiest building in the EU. At 114 metres above the scurrying pedestrians and toy-sized trains of London Bridge, Aqua's one of the most altitudinous bars in London, and it's the spectacular floor-to-ceiling vista that make it worth the trip up in the lift. All 32 boroughs (plus the City) spread out around in a gloriously elaborate panoply of streets, tower blocks, parks, churches, railway lines and countless iconic structures to point out. Every seat comes with something different and endlessly fascinating to look at – which makes Aqua an ideal spot if you're worried conversation might dry up...

ESSENTIAL ORDER The inventive tea-based cocktails are a cut above – try Heaven On Earth, with aged rum, sherry, tangerine and pistachio maple syrup.

Level 31, The Shard, 31 St Thomas Street, Borough, SE1 9RY.

☎ *020 3011 1256*

🖥 *www.aquashard.co.uk*

⊖ *Borough tube.*

● FRANK'S CAFÉ

Drink... in an art-filled concrete car park with a view.

Ten floors up in a deserted car park in Peckham... It doesn't sound like the setting for one of London's most consistently cool bars, but scale the heights and you'll be rewarded with not only large-scale new sculpture works on the way up, but an arresting panorama of the city from an unusual aspect when you arrive at the top. The downside, so to speak: it's only open over the summer months and is open to the elements – dress accordingly.

ESSENTIAL ORDER Simple cocktails, simple food – a Negroni, ox-heart skewers. *Tenth floor, Peckham Multistorey Car Park, 95a Rye Lane, Peckham, SE15 4ST.* 🖳 *www.frankscafe.org.uk* ⊖ *Peckham Rye Overground.*

● THE SHIP

Drink... in the finest Thames-side pub till Oxford.
The Ship has been serving thirsty Wandsworth
workers since it opened as a riverside inn in 1786,
but the eighteenth-century waterman might not
recognise it nowadays, especially in summer. Despite
the unpromising location next to a cement-landing
wharf, it's massively popular – the cosy and quiet
public bar has been augmented with a conservatory,
restaurant and impressive beer garden complete
with its own bar; there can't be many pubs with the
space to pack in so many drinkers and puts them all
in solid sight of the upstream Thames.
ESSENTIAL ORDER Sambrook's Wandle –
a refreshing south London ale that goes hand-in-
hand with sunshine and water.
41 Jews Row, Wandsworth Town, SW18 1TB.
☎ *020 8870 9667* 🖳 *www.theship.co.uk*
⊖ *Wandsworth Town rail.*

● THE LITTLE BAR

Drink... in a less-than-large local you'll long to live near.

By the time you leave this diminutive Tooting drinkery you'll probably want to open your own little bar. How hard can it be, you'll think – but Little Bar makes it look easy. Everything seems to suit the size – the small list of cocktails, spirits, beers, ciders and wines is clearly chosen with great consideration, and there are platefuls of cheese and charcuterie. Grab one of the stools and before long you'll probably get to know the chatty staff too.

ESSENTIAL ORDER Negronis are a speciality: have an 'Unusual' one with Hendrick's gin.

145 Mitcham Road, Tooting, SW17 9PE.
☎ *020 8672 7317*
⊖ *Tooting Broadway tube.*

● THE MAYFLOWER

Drink... with your feet in the Thames.
On a peaceful stretch of the river,
in tucked-away Rotherhithe, is this
picturesque and historic little pub. It
would be special even if it was solidly
on dry land, but it backs right on to the
Thames: stand on the wooden deck
projecting over the water and watch the
wash slap against the pillars below. It's
particularly pleasing at night, when the
towers of the City sparkle in the distance.
Inside is equally attractive – there's
a fire, wooden pews, framed antique
manuscripts and various pertinent
mottos inscribed on the walls.
An enchanting place.
ESSENTIAL ORDER Take a mulled wine
and a blanket (both provided!) outside on
a dark and chilly evening and watch the
riverboats speed by.
117 Rotherhithe Street,
Rotherhithe, SE16 4NF.
☎ *020 7237 4088*
🖥 *www.mayflowerpub.co.uk*
⊖ *Rotherhithe Overground.*

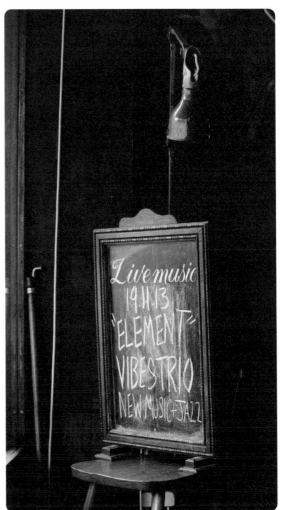

● CABLE CAFE

Drink... in a perfect noir of a bar.
At night, this singular little spot is one of the most atmospheric hideaways in London. Beside a neon manual coffee machine and below old railway station lamps, couples chat in hushed tones and lone readers repose like Left Bank poets against a soundtrack of mellifluent jazz. The tobacco-brown wood walls are dotted with various vintage bits and pieces, bands sometimes play in a corner, there's no written menu, mobile phones somehow seem inappropriate. A place to lose yourself for a while.
ESSENTIAL ORDER Something strong, neat and Continental – how about a Campari on ice (or even a double espresso)?
8 Brixton Road, Kennington, SW9 6BU.
☎ *020 8617 9629*
⊖ *Oval tube.*

● THE HARWOOD ARMS

Drink... among the rolling fields and country lanes of Fulham.
This pretty and elegantly scuffed place pushes the boundaries of what can be called a pub. One can indeed sit and just order a drink, but the set tables and attentive waiters leave no doubt that this is a gastropub. And not just any gastropub: Fulhamites flock here for the Michelin-starred food, much of which is game shot in the Home Counties (see the monochrome portraits on the walls of hunting parties and be left in no doubt where your plateful came from). Drinkers can tuck into bar snacks – roe deer and walnut terrine, say. A pack of peanuts will never again suffice.
ESSENTIAL ORDER The elegant wines by the glass go down rather nicely with a soft-yolked venison Scotch egg.
Walham Grove, Fulham, SW6 1QP.
☎ *020 7386 1847*
🖥 *www.harwoodarms.com*
⊖ *West Brompton tube.*

ESSENTIAL ORDER That old Polynesian favourite, the Zombie, comes with nine rums, spiced syrup, cherry, absinthe and lime.
177 Portobello Road, Notting Hill, W11 2DY.
☎ *020 7041 9833*
🖳 *www.trailerhappiness.com*
⊖ *Ladbroke Grove tube.*

● BAD SPORTS

Drink... in a cool-kitsch Mexican pastiche.
The sports bar – the curiously American institution that seems right at home in Austin or Kalamazoo, but never quite works as an export, despite its simple elements: drink, screens showing sports, easy food. Bad Sports has those things, but because it's in hip Hackney Road, it does it with a pinch of salt – which makes it work brilliantly. No one's really there to watch gridiron, they're there to eat the fabulous tacos and drink the fabulous cocktails, which aren't sophisticated (think a frozen banana daiquiri or one that includes a shot of a notorious monk-made tonic wine popular in Scotland), but they taste amazing and they're fun – which is often more important.
ESSENTIAL ORDER The Coatbridge Negroni, which replaces the vermouth with Buckfast. It's better than it sounds!
184 Hackney Road, Hoxton, E2 7QL.
☎ *020 7033 3868* 🖳 *www.badsports.co.uk*
⊖ *Hoxton Overground.*

● TRAILER HAPPINESS

Drink... in a '70s Hawaiian beach lounge.
Three wines, three beers, but barrel-loads of rum
– this Notting Hill basement bar is all about totally tropical cocktails to be drank with tongue in cheek (one contains Ribena). It's on the tiki side of tacky, with groovy patterned wallpaper, Eero Aarnio-style armchairs and wallfuls of JH Lynch 'Tina' prints. A riot.

TICK INDEX

- ☐ 7 Tales p132
- ☐ American Bar at the Stafford p105
- ☐ Aqua Shard p160
- ☐ Artesian p131
- ☐ The Auld Shillelagh p151
- ☐ Bad Sports p170
- ☐ Bar Américain p24
- ☐ The Bar at the Goring p116
- ☐ Bar Termini p124
- ☐ The Beaufort Bar and the American Bar at the Savoy p101
- ☐ The Black Friar p107
- ☐ Black Rock p128
- ☐ Blue Posts p150
- ☐ Boisdale p135
- ☐ The Book Club p155
- ☐ Booking Office p112
- ☐ Brewdog p80
- ☐ The Bricklayer's Arms p55
- ☐ The Bull p73
- ☐ Cable Cafe p167
- ☐ Camden Town Brewery Bar p74
- ☐ The Carpenter's Arms p52
- ☐ Cask p70
- ☐ The Charles Lamb p45
- ☐ The Clapton Hart p51

- ☐ Coburg Bar at the Connaught p22
- ☐ Cocktail Lounge at the Zetter Townhouse p17
- ☐ Coupette p32
- ☐ Craft Beer Co p69
- ☐ Crate Brewery p83
- ☐ The Crown & Anchor p84
- ☐ The Dove, W6 p118
- ☐ The Dove, E8 p78
- ☐ Draft House p89
- ☐ Duke's p106
- ☐ The Earl of Essex p75
- ☐ Euston Tap p70
- ☐ Experimental Cocktail Club p14
- ☐ The Faltering Fullback p159
- ☐ Frank's Café p162
- ☐ The French House p96
- ☐ The George Inn p115
- ☐ The Grenadier p57
- ☐ Happiness Forgets p31
- ☐ Harp p66
- ☐ The Harwood Arms p168
- ☐ Hawkes Cidery & Taproom p79
- ☐ Hawksmoor p34
- ☐ The Holly Bush p111
- ☐ Howling Hops p87

- [ ] The Ivy House   p56
- [ ] Jamaica Wine House   p110
- [ ] Jerusalem Tavern   p67
- [ ] Jose   p135
- [ ] Kensington Wine Rooms   p142
- [ ] The Little Bar   p164
- [ ] London Cocktail Club   p14
- [ ] **The Lord Tredegar**   **p43**
- [ ] Lounge Bohemia   p137
- [ ] Mark's Bar   p29
- [ ] The Mayflower   **p165**
- [ ] Mayor of Scaredy Cat Town   **p158**
- [ ] Milk & Honey   p20
- [ ] Mr Fogg's   **p149**
- [ ] **The Nag's Head**   p60
- [ ] Nightjar   p30
- [ ] **Paradise by Way of Kensal Green**   p59
- [ ] **The Pineapple**   p45
- [ ] Portobello Star   p141
- [ ] The Pride of Spitalfields   p154
- [ ] **The Prince Alfred**   p119
- [ ] **The Princess Louise**   p102
- [ ] **The Prospect of Whitby**   p114
- [ ] Punch Room   p23
- [ ] **The Queen's Head**   **p42**
- [ ] **The Railway Tavern Ale House**   p49

- [ ] The Rake   p88
- [ ] **The Royal Oak**   p84
- [ ] Rules   p99
- [ ] Rum Kitchen   p138
- [ ] Sager + Wilde   **p138**
- [ ] Scottish Stores   p152
- [ ] Scout   p37
- [ ] The Ship   p163
- [ ] Shochu Lounge   p130
- [ ] **The Southampton Arms**   p77
- [ ] Super Lyan   p20
- [ ] **Swift**   p36
- [ ] **The Sun Tavern**   p136
- [ ] Terroirs   p124
- [ ] Three Sheets   p27
- [ ] Trailer Happiness   **p170**
- [ ] Untitled   p18
- [ ] Vinoteca   p127
- [ ] Well & Bucket   p157
- [ ] **The Wenlock Arms**   p46
- [ ] **The White Horse**   p90
- [ ] Worship Street Whistling Shop   **p36**
- [ ] Ye Olde Cheshire Cheese   p98
- [ ] Ye Olde Mitre   p109

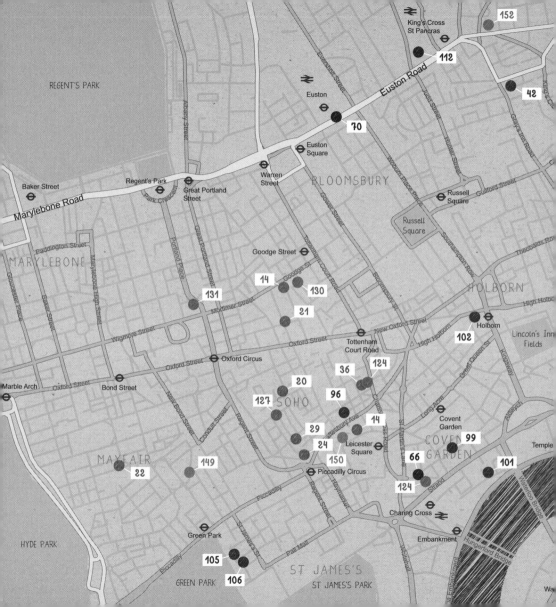

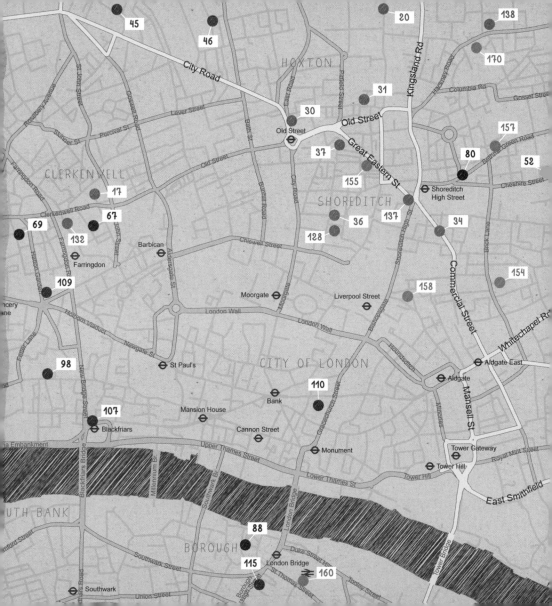

Brimming with creative inspiration, how-to projects and useful
information to enrich your everyday life, Quarto Knows is a
favourite destination for those pursuing their interests and passions.
Visit our site and dig deeper with our books into your area of
interest: Quarto Creates, Quarto Cooks, Quarto Homes, Quarto
Lives, Quarto Drives, Quarto Explores, Quarto Gifts, or Quarto Kids.

MIX
Paper from
responsible sources
FSC® C104723